THE MAGIK OF

SATAN

MASTERING LIGHT AND DARKNESS

DAVID THOMPSON

THE MAGIK OF

SATAN

MASTERING LIGHT AND DARKNESS

DAVID THOMPSON

HIGH MAGIK BOOK 14

* TRANS MUNDANE *
PUBLISHING
—— OCCULT KNOWLEDGE ——

To Angela, an authentic and powerful satanist if I ever saw one.

To Lilith, for her help this past year.

To Fortuna, for always being around, but not in a stalkerish way.

"We must remember that Satan has his miracles, too."

John Calvin

Disclaimer

The contents of this book, "The Magik of Satan," are for informational and educational purposes only. The information provided within this book should not be considered as a substitute for legal, financial, psychological, medical, or any other form of professional advice.

This book is intended to provide insights into the magik associated with Satan, based on esoteric and occult literature. Though magik is a powerful force, it should be handled responsibly. The author cannot be held accountable for any misuse or unintended consequences arising from the practice of the magik described herein. It is the reader's responsibility to exercise discernment, caution, and to consult appropriate professionals for advice tailored to their individual circumstances. All information in this book is provided "as is".

By accessing, reading, or using any part of this book, you agree that you are solely responsible for your own actions, and you explicitly release the author, David Thompson, and any affiliated parties, from any liability for any negative consequences that may result from applying the information found within this book.

This disclaimer is subject to change without notice and was last updated on the date of publication of this book. If you do not agree with this disclaimer, please do not read, use, or implement any of the information provided in "The Magik of Satan."

TABLE OF CONTENTS

AUTHOR'S NOTE

When I first began this book, I was looking at a rather short, and light, book on Satan. A bit of good-natured humor, maybe a few horrible puns... but it evolved. Oh man, did it evolve.

I know I'm a bit long-winded when I get wound up, and this book really made me stop, and consider how I was putting this together. Satan himself didn't help.

You see, being a psychic, I can hear the spirits. And man, I got an ear-full with Satan. As I was working the outline, my original six chapters got an additional five chapters tacked onto it. Plus, the pathworking material. I put all of those into their own chapter at the end. This way, those of you who're somewhat eager to try this, you can turn to that section and begin work. But you'll be skipping the sections on precautions. You see, Satan is a known trickster. Yes, Lord of Lies. So, without preparing properly, taking precautions, and just diving in, you are setting yourself up for some interesting times.

But Satan is also a gentleman. He'll be nice, but check to make sure he doesn't have his fingers crossed behind his back.

I know, I do this myself. I'll get a new book on a topic I'm eager to learn, and I'll skim the first few chapters, going "Yeah, yeah.. And?" And wouldn't you know it, after all my experience, I'll still skip ahead and totally miss an important aspect and the magik sputters, if I'm lucky.

As many books that I have written, I must have read double that in other author's books. Some, well, most, just dive right into the rituals, and I have discovered quite a few leave out important bits. This happens quite a bit with books on the more publically acceptable term "Manifestation" or "Law of Attraction". Not a thing wrong with either of those two subjects. Hell, I have several books lined up for release on that subject later 2024. (Hey - go to the About section and sign up for my newsletter!!! That's where you'll first hear about any new book!) However, I was using real magik long before the "Secret" was written. Yet, I also read that book and the companion books, plus books on channeling this stuff. It all seems to follow a similar trajectory, to make actual magik acceptable for the masses. Especially the people in the United States, who view magik with the same suspicion as a Puritan in Salem, Massachusetts in the mid-1600s.

The rituals in this book will be a slight departure from my previous books. Sure, I'll have the usual presentation for many of the rituals, but I have also crafted many rituals in a more "readable" fashion, limiting my use of a "ritual template". They're still easy to follow, easy to work, but are written a bit differently.

In reality, Satan himself, once you get to know him, is actually a very sophisticated, well-behaved gentleman. Of all this material, we'll only look at the Egregore aspect briefly. He has so much else to offer.

So, this is it. 13 total chapters, rituals covering everything from achieving fame, accumulating wealth, attracting love, shadow work, controlling others, empowerment, healing, healthy weight, pacts and pathworking. My biggest book to date. I go into some detail with his history, which I feel is needed to place this complex spirit into the right context.

Okay. Enough chatter, time for some magik!

Enjoy!

CALL ME STAN

The sultry heart of Mississippi during the mid-1930s,

A skinny young man, in clothes a bit too small. This is Tommy, a fledgling jazz guitarist. After hitchhiking from New Orleans, he now found himself walking down a dusty road. The moon hung low, casting elongated shadows of ancient trees across his path. He was dressed in a worn blue suit, a faded white stained shirt, and a wide-brimmed hat, shadowing his determined eyes. His guitar, a weathered extension of his soul, hung on his back. Tommy was heading to the infamous crossroads, the place of legends, where it was said one could trade their soul for musical greatness.

As the clock struck midnight, Tommy reached the crossroads. He expected something ominous, but all he found was the tranquil Southern night, the chirping of crickets, and a gentle breeze. Then, out of the shadows stepped a man in a black suit, his skin a subtle shade of reddish bronze, his eyes deep and understanding. He had no horns, no pitchfork – nothing that screamed the brimstone tales Tommy had heard. This man, with an air of elegance and an enigmatic smile, sat on a tree stump and motioned for Tommy to join him.

"Howdy, suh," Tommy stammered. It was obvious he was nervous. "Are you who I think you are, suh?"

"Folks call me many names, but you can call me Stan," he said, his voice smooth like molasses. "Here, sit down, please."

Tommy, uncertain yet intrigued, sat down opposite him. Stan opened his satchel, pulling out a bottle of fine whiskey and two glasses. He poured the amber liquid, offering one to Tommy.

"This is some good stuff." Stan remarked, taking a slow sip. A slow smile flickered across his red lips. He closed his eyes as the whiskey slid down his throat. He opened his eyes and fixed Tommy with a steady gaze. "Tell me why you're here, young man."

Tommy sat a moment. He looked into his glass, then back up at Stan. Trembling, he lifted the glass to his lips, and tasted the fine liquor.

"I want to be the greatest jazz guitarist, maybe even a famous blues singer," Tommy replied, his voice a mix of hope and desperation. He kept his head down, avoiding eye contact.

Stan chuckled softly, shaking his head. "Ah, the dreams of youth. But do you know what it truly takes to achieve such dreams?"

Tommy nodded, "I was told you could help... for a price."

Stan's eyes gleamed with a mixture of sadness and wisdom. "Tommy, the stories you've heard about souls traded and dark deals, they're just that – stories. I'm no soul collector. I'm more of a... misunderstood guide."

As the night deepened, Stan spoke of his own story, how he had been misrepresented in scriptures and literature. He talked about the beauty and complexity of life, the misunderstood aspects of his character, and the true nature of his existence.

"People fear what they don't understand," Stan said, "and they often make demons out of the unknown."

Tommy listened, captivated. This wasn't the conversation he expected. It was a revelation, a new perspective on an old tale.

"And what about my dream?" Tommy finally asked.

Stan smiled, setting his glass down. "To achieve greatness in music, or in any art, practice is your true deal at the crossroads. It's dedication, passion, and the relentless pursuit of your craft. No mystical deal can give you what time, effort, and heart can."

The first light of dawn began to creep across the sky as they talked. Tommy realized that he had been searching for a shortcut, but real success required something more profound and personal.

As the sun rose, casting a warm glow over the crossroads, Stan stood up, his figure now just a man against the light of a new day. "Remember, Tommy, greatness comes from within. And it's not just about the notes you play, but the life you pour into them. To play cool, you have to be hot. To play hot, you got to be cool, understand?"

With those parting words, Stan disappeared into the shadows of an enormous oak tree as mysteriously as he had arrived, leaving Tommy alone with his thoughts and his guitar. Tommy felt a newfound sense of purpose and clarity. He picked up his guitar, playing a few chords that resonated with the truth he had just learned. Like magik, his fingers picked out a nonatonic blues scale, which made him smile.

He then walked to the roadside; his thumb outstretched. A truck stopped, and he hopped in, heading towards Jacksonville. In his heart, he carried a secret of the crossroads – it wasn't about deals with the devil, but about meeting oneself.

Years later, Tommy would become a renowned blues singer, his music rich with the soulful depth of his journey. And at every performance, he would remember that night at the crossroads, where he met not a devil, but a guide who showed him the real path to his dreams.

INTRODUCTION

Prince of Darkness.

Lord of Lies.

Among all the spirits in magik, whether it be High Magik or any other form, there are only a few names that have the ability to evoke such intense fear, spread so much misinformation, and provoke such a wide range of opinions as that of Satan. However, in his favor, you do get what you expect when you summon his Holy Darkness.

Notice I said "Expect." If you feel, deep down inside, a different desire than what you asked for, guess which will be delivered? Working with Satan demands you confront your inner "Satan", so to speak, and make sure your petition actually reflects what you truly desire. If your desire is nebulous, undefined, or loaded with restrictions, it just won't happen the way you want it to happen.

This is what makes Satan difficult to work with. It's not actually Satan, you see, but your own inner indecisiveness that is pumping the brakes on the manifestation of your desire.

Satan has captivated the religious, philosophical, and cultural imagination for centuries, evolving into a multidimensional character that defies simple categorization. Yet, a multitude of misconceptions persist, reducing Satan to a mere symbol of evil, corruption, and malevolence. This introduction aims to dismantle some of the prevailing "mythconceptions" that obscure the complex nuances of Satan in both history and high magik.

One of the most widespread fallacies is viewing Satan solely as the epitome of evil incarnate. Conventional religious narratives, especially within the Christian framework, often portray him as a malevolent force diametrically opposed to God. While it's true that in these narratives, Satan acts as the adversary, his role transcends mere antagonism. In Hebrew tradition, for instance, "Ha-Satan" operates as an accuser or tester, a function that is integral to moral and spiritual maturation. Even within the context of Christian theology, Satan raises complex questions about duality, free will, and the essence of sin.

Another frequent mistake is the indiscriminate confusion of Satan with Lucifer. Although pop culture often fuses the two, they emanate from different origins. "Lucifer," the "bringer of light" or "morning star," symbolizes enlightenment and individualistic pursuit. His conflation with Satan primarily arises from literary interpretations like John Milton's "Paradise Lost," which is an inventive work, not a religious text.

The notion of Satan is not uniform across all religious and philosophical landscapes. In Islam, the figure of Iblis plays a role akin to Satan, but carries unique traits and origin stories. In Eastern philosophies like Buddhism, entities like Mara serve similar but not identical functions to Satan. Projecting the concept of Satan as a universal archetype across varied belief systems culminates in an overly simplified and Eurocentric perspective.

Modern media further perpetuates these mythconceptions, often linking Satanic figures or symbols to malevolent supernatural activities or criminal enterprises. The infamous "Satanic Panic" of the 1980s stands as a glaring example where sensationalism led to a rampant misconception that Satanic cults were engaging in widespread ritual abuse.

In high magik, misunderstandings flourish as well. Just start a discussion as to the proper way to pronounce an ENN, and it'll descend into a flame war within hours. Satan is a significant figure in Left-Hand Path traditions, but this by no means implies that its practitioners engage in malevolent or unethical deeds. The Left-Hand Path focuses on individualism, self-deification, and personal empowerment, utilizing Satan as an archetype rather than an object of orthodox worship.

Given the intricate history and multiple interpretations of Satan, reducing him to a singular villainous caricature diminishes the richness of the traditions in which he plays a part. A more nuanced comprehension can offer profound insights into the dual nature of existence, the paradox of free will, and the labyrinthine facets of the human psyche. Whether examined as a religious entity, a mythological archetype, or a focal point in high magik, Satan resists simplistic labels. Dispelling the "mythconceptions" surrounding him not only corrects his distorted portrayal but also deepens our understanding of the spiritual, religious, or philosophical systems that incorporate this enigmatic figure.

It gets worse when you realize that the horn hand gesture, appropriated by heavy metal fans, is actually a school hand symbol for the University of Texas Longhorns. The "Hook 'em Horns" hand gesture is a symbol of school pride and spirit for the University of Texas at Austin. It was introduced on November 11, 1955, during a pep rally on the eve of the annual football game against their arch-rival, Texas A&M University. The sign was created by Harley Clark Jr., who was the head cheerleader at the time. He claims to have been inspired by the school's mascot, Bevo the Longhorn, as the hand sign mimics the steer's horns. The gesture is made by extending the index and pinky fingers while holding the middle and ring fingers down with the thumb, resembling a longhorn's silhouette.

This gesture quickly became an iconic representation for the University of Texas, and it is used widely during sports events, school functions, and even as a not-so-secret sign of greeting among members of the UT community. It has seeped into the broader culture as a symbol of Texan identity and is frequently seen at events beyond just university-related activities.

Interestingly, the "Hook 'em Horns" hand gesture has also attracted some controversy and misinterpretation. In some cultures, the same or similar hand gestures have different meanings that can range from offensive to symbolic of the devil. However, in the context of the University of Texas, the "Hook 'em Horns" hand sign remains a benign and beloved emblem of school pride.

I'm also a graduate of the University of Texas at Austin. I learned this gesture well before I learned the other useful hand gestures.

In this book, I'll explore various aspects of Satan, and each set of rituals I have in this book will summon a specific aspect best suited for the ritual.

Many of these aspects you might have heard about, and many books seem to focus on only one or two aspects. Here's a list of aspects I've discovered, and this list is not in any way complete. I won't cover rituals to them all, but I'll list these here. You are free to summon any of these aspects using my methods. Just alter the ritual where needed.

Rebellion and Freedom: Perhaps the most recognized aspect of Satan is as a symbol of rebellion. This represents the defiance of conventional norms and the courage to challenge authority. In many magikal practices, invoking Satan is seen as an act of embracing one's own power and the freedom to follow one's own path.

Transformation and Enlightenment: Satan is also seen as a bringer of enlightenment, akin to Prometheus bringing fire to humanity. This aspect involves the pursuit of knowledge, often forbidden or hidden, and the transformative power of that knowledge. Enlightenment is my personal life goal, and this starts by rejecting dogma society places upon us in our current lives.

Testing and Adversity: In many traditions, Satan is viewed as a tester or adversary. Rather than being an embodiment of evil, this aspect represents the challenges and obstacles that lead to greater strength and wisdom. Working with Satan in this context means seeking the fortitude to overcome personal trials and tribulations.

Material Mastery and Earthly Power: Satan is often associated with material wealth and earthly power. This aspect involves the mastery over the physical world and the ability to manifest one's desires in the material realm. Think income and wealth magik.

Individuation and Self-Realization: In the context of Jungian psychology, Satan can represent the shadow self, encompassing the parts of one's identity that are repressed or unacknowledged. Engaging with this aspect involves a deep dive into self-awareness and personal growth.

Sexuality and Liberation: Satan is also often associated with sexual energy and the breaking of sexual taboos. This aspect embraces the acceptance of natural desires and the breaking free from societal restraints regarding sexuality. You know the ultra-religious folks hate this aspect. This is because using this aspect will break one free of the social constraints placed upon sexuality. Imagine a gender fluid person trapped in our society. This aspect will help one accept their sexuality, enabling them to move on.

Balance of Light and Darkness: In some beliefs, Satan represents the necessary balance between light and darkness. This duality is crucial for understanding the full spectrum of human experience and the universe.

Egregore: This aspect is the most known, and used, aspect of Satan. This is the aspect you get when using his Daemonic ENN (a sort of summoning, comprised of words of a mixed language, which means nothing to most people but summons a specific daemon, or in this case, an aspect of a daemon).

Each of these aspects offers a different lens through which to understand and work with the figure of Satan in magikal practices. They reflect a complex and often paradoxical character, far removed from the simplistic embodiment of evil as often portrayed in mainstream narratives. Engaging with these different aspects can provide a deeper, more nuanced understanding of Satan's role in various spiritual and magikal systems.

In this book, I also depart from setting out just rituals. In some subjects, I'll also include simple spells as well. It will vary, as some aspects of Satan shouldn't ever be worked outside a protective circle.

So, let's begin with "The Magik of Satan - Mastering Light and Darkness."

CHAPTER 1

CHANNELED HISTORY

After a long channeling session with Satan, here's what I have come up with.

Among all the information about the early years of the human experiment on Earth, we encounter the story of how Thoth/Hermes assisted in the creation of Atlantis. In some tales, the energy that destroyed the previous civilization was termed "Satanic" energy. Satanic energy is closely aligned with a masculine energy, which shifts the population away from mental technology (such as magik) towards a physical, technological system, which can cause havoc.

In the scope of this story, which is only partially true, we see the initial use of the energy of Satan as energy that can destroy, as well as create. This story appears to have connected the being we call Satan, in an egregore aspect, with the energy of this event - and I am now unable to find the original material for this at the time of this book.

This is only one of multiple stories in the occult community of the establishment of the current civilization. In the ones I have researched and channeled, most gods/goddess, daemons, and genius spirits originate as immortal masters from a few civilizations before the current one.

Slowly, modern archaeologists (standard school types) are finding evidence of much earlier, technologically advanced societies, such as Gobekli Tepe and others. Massive stones and massive temples, purposely buried to preserve them for the future. Even evidence of living underground during worldwide cataclysmic events, such as the possible impact of a comet or asteroid, called the Younger-Drays event.

What this has to do with Satan?

Well, it kinda obscures his true origin. His origin as a spirit seems to be in the traditional texts of the Abrahamic religions, beginning with YHWH and his followers. (*There is some information that old YHWH was a being of extraterrestrial origin. I'm not touching that in this book.)

So, upon contacting Satan in his overall aspect, a combination of all the aspects in this book, I get: "I began in the maelstrom of the creation event itself, as we all did. I did not incarnate as you define it, I attached myself to several species of sentient beings, eventually finding myself in your star system. I saw the early experiments with the species called human. As I touched their spirits, I was asked by the persona you call "God" or "Jehovah" to assist in testing the early humans to make sure the hijacking of their spirits was working as intended during the early mystical events as chronicled in the holy books of these people. Previously, these pitiful beings were altered after the original progenitors had left them on their own, for whatever purposes our real creator had in mind. From this, I had multiple faces. That aspect of myself, that of a provoking spirit, was useful for these early beings who sought to control these humans. Upon reflection, I know someone had to be the scapegoat of the hijacking of these people, and thus, I became the symbol of what they called 'evil'.

"After communication with the being that is actually the creator, I joined with the other spirits in an attempt to be of some use to enlightened humans on this planet. The hijacking was in error, having been misled by the spirits calling themselves your "god".

"I have many aspects, or faces, and I am now here for you all, all humans."

At this point, I now turn to the recorded history of this fascinating spirit.

THE HISTORY OF SATAN

Before we plunge into the labyrinth of magik, myths, and misconceptions, let's rewind the threads of time to one of his earliest mentions: Ha-Satan in Hebrew tradition. Yes, the tale is thick with intricacies and subtexts, like a bewitched forest hiding both boons and banes. And as much as Satan himself relishes a hearty laugh, we'll find room for a chuckle or two amid these weighty matters.

Firstly, "Ha-Satan" isn't a name; it's a title. In Hebrew, it means 'The Accuser' or 'The Adversary.' Sounds like a courtroom drama, doesn't it? Imagine this scenario: God, the indescribable Creator, finds Himself in need of a celestial prosecutor, an individual who can assess the righteousness of His creations. That's when Ha-Satan enters the picture, but not as the typical horned and red-skinned caricature we often associate with him. Instead, Ha-Satan appears as an angelic figure, exuding dignity and completely devoted to fulfilling his duty. He's not hell-bent on bringing the downfall of humanity, but focused on testing its mettle. It's his job, and someone's got to do it.

Pause and consider this for a moment: Satan started as a kind of divine quality control. It sounds less glamorous when put that way, but don't let the apparent banality fool you. Remember, the Hebrew understanding of this figure contributes an astonishing layer to the eventual conceptualization of Satan. So don't shortchange the celestial prosecutor; he's pivotal to understanding this energy.

Take the biblical tale of Job, where Ha-Satan literally places a cosmic bet with God about the steadfastness of a human soul. Could there be anything more riveting than this divine wager? God boasts about how loyal and upright Job is, and Ha-Satan, ever the professional skeptic, responds, "Oh, really? Let's put that to the test, shall we?" What follows is a series of trials that would make any mortal quiver, but it's all part of the process—a celestial audit, if you will.

Imagine being the subject of a divine bet. One day you're tending your fields, content and joyous, and the next, you're the centerpiece in a cosmic examination of human resilience and faith. The notion is both thrilling and terrifying, like riding a roller-coaster designed by philosophers and archangels.

Satan's role in Job's trials illustrates a fascinating point: he wasn't acting out of malice but fulfilling his duty, sanctioned by the Creator Himself. While later interpretations draped him in diabolical motifs, the foundational framework considered him an essential part of the divine bureaucracy. Think of him as a supernatural civil servant with a dash of celestial panache.

Oh, and this concept of a pair of powerful people making a bet to use a less powerful person is the subject of several movies.

Another thing worth noting—though Ha-Satan is often identified with temptation, his role in Hebrew tradition is more nuanced. He's not handing out poisoned apples or signing Faustian pacts; he's essentially asking questions that need to be asked, probing human motives and actions like a skilled interrogator. You know those introspective moments when you question your actions, motives, or the moral fabric of your being? It's almost like a mini court trial in your head, isn't it? Well, guess who you can thank for that internal courtroom drama.

You may be tempted to draw a line connecting the Hebrew Ha-Satan to the devil of later Christian tradition, but resist the urge. This is one instance where drawing lines can lead you down a slippery slope to oversimplification, and we can't have that. Instead, picture a tapestry with threads of various hues—some dark, some radiant—all contributing to the complex figure that Satan eventually becomes. And don't worry, we're going to follow each of those threads as we progress, but remember, it all starts here, with an angelic prosecutor in the heavenly courts.

Intrigued? Good, because you're being led down a rabbit hole, not of diabolical schemes, but of profound insights and startling revelations about a figure that has been severely misunderstood. After all, the first step to wisdom is the dismantling of ignorance. So, buckle up, because this is merely the foreword in a sprawling epic that stretches from the courts of Heaven to the shadowy corners of human consciousness. And yes, even to the clandestine circles of magik where his name is invoked in hushed whispers and elaborate rituals.

Now that we have explored the intricate and complex origins of Satan in Hebrew tradition. However, before we conclude, there is additional information that I would like to share. The interesting history of Old Nick becomes more and more interesting the deeper into this rabbit warren we go.

It's not JUST the Old or New Testament. This history gets really weird, as well, but rest assured, there will be chuckles along the way. Satan, as we know, has a wicked sense of humor.

Okay - so let's all get dressed up and go to Sunday School. (No gum, unless you bring enough for everyone.)

Christian Interpretations: The Old Testament Rewind

Before we leap into the New Testament, let's twirl the dial back to the Old Testament, which Christians adopted and expanded upon. Yes, the Hebrew Ha-Satan makes guest appearances here, but these aren't reruns. The Old Testament, when viewed through Christian lenses, adds a tint of impending doom to the character. Here, Satan transitions from a divine quality-controller to a more autonomous entity. Still no horns or pitchfork, but we're getting closer to the figure who could merit a top spot on the FBI's celestial Most Wanted list.

Remember the serpent in the Garden of Eden? While the Hebrew tradition doesn't directly name the snake as Satan, Christians embraced the idea wholeheartedly. Yes, that serpent, a truly cunning creature! It's here that Satan takes on a more devious role—no longer just questioning and accusing, but nudging, tempting, and, well, downright deceiving. No wonder apples got a bad rap for eternity! (Not to mention creating the idea of "original Sin", thus dooming all humans, then blaming it on the woman. This story only serves further establish the male-dominated religions for the rest of our history.)

Think of that serpent like the slick talker at a cosmic party, the one who convinces you to try 'just one shot' of divine knowledge. The next thing you know, you're getting kicked out of paradise, and the bouncer is an angel with a flaming sword. Thanks, Satan!

Actually, it gets murkier as you go along, because many Rabbinical texts suggest the tempter serpent in the garden was actually Lilith. It's as if they simply cannot make up their minds who the real bad guy is, and never once did they look at themselves.

THE NEW TESTAMENT REVEAL

Now, let take a look at the what is called The "New Testament," which is essentially a sequel to the Torah, featuring a new protagonist. Of course, the new hero needed an anti-hero, thus His Unholiness.

Here's where our leading man, now playing the role of a proper villain, gains new layers and motivations. We see him tempting Christ in the desert, a high-stakes scene where the very soul of mankind hangs in the balance. If Satan succeeds, it's not just a score for Team Inferno; it's a cosmic upheaval of divine plans.

Imagine being Jesus, fasting for 40 days, hungry and alone, and along comes this well-articulated entity offering you the world on a silver platter. It's like being on a diet and someone waving a delicious chocolate cake under your nose. Satan, at this point, isn't merely an accuser; he's a tempter with cosmic consequences. Yet, despite the high stakes, Jesus says 'no thanks' to the devilish offers, leaving Satan to reevaluate his life choices, so to speak.

Let's not forget the celestial soap opera's grand finale—the Book of Revelation. Satan morphs from mere tempter to a bona fide dragon, ready to wage war in heaven. I mean, talk about a character shift! He's no longer just the accuser or the tempter; he's the embodiment of cosmic rebellion. It's like he went from being a court prosecutor to leading an insurrection, all while sporting scales and breathing fire. You can't make this stuff up. Well, actually, they did make this stuff up, but that's what makes it so irresistible.

Revelation doesn't just stop at war; it promises an eventual downfall for our anti-hero, complete with chains and a bottomless pit. It's a cliffhanger that has kept humanity on the edge of its collective seat for millennia. Just how will it all pan out? Will Satan return for a redemptive arc, or is he destined to play the villain for eternity?

As you may have gathered by now, the Christian narrative takes the complexity of Satan and amplifies it, enriching it with new roles, motivations, and a peppering of divine drama. Whether you view him as an antagonist in a cosmic tale or as a misunderstood anti-hero, one thing's for sure—this celestial being knows how to keep things interesting.

So there you have it, a whirlwind tour of Satan's evolving roles in Christian theology, each more tantalizing than the last. You're not ready to quit now, are you? Of course not. Because just ahead lies the labyrinthine world of magik, where the misunderstood accuser takes center stage as an enigmatic guide, mentor, and yes, trickster.

Take a breath, maybe grab a snack or a cup of tea, and let's continue. I'm just getting to the good parts.

Hey everyone, I just wanted to remind you that we still have a lot of tasks to complete, so let's continue pushing forward. Although we have already explored Hebrew texts and enjoyed Christian narratives, let us continue our intellectual journey. I now want to cover and look into the Islamic perspectives and pay homage to Eastern figures, who bears a striking resemblance to our multifaceted protagonist.

THE ISLAMIC CHAPTER: MEET IBLIS AND SHAYTAN

When examining the expansive framework of Islamic theology, one cannot overlook the substantial and intricate role played by Iblis. Known in Islamic lore as the counterpart to Satan, Iblis's story is one of rebellion, pride, and an enduring vendetta against humanity. This narrative begins in a celestial setting, where Iblis, once a favored being among the angels, finds himself at a pivotal crossroads of divine command and personal conviction.

The pivotal moment that defines Iblis' fate unfolds with the creation of Adam. As God introduces this new being, formed from clay, a decree is issued to the celestial inhabitants to bow in recognition of this creation. Iblis, fashioned from smokeless fire, perceives this directive as a slight to his superior nature. This isn't just a refusal to acknowledge a fellow creation; it's a statement of defiance, born from a sense of pride and superiority. Imagine the internal turmoil, the clash of loyalty and ego, as Iblis grapples with the command to bow to what he perceives as a lesser being. His refusal marks not just disobedience, but a declaration of personal autonomy that ultimately leads to his fall from grace.

This act of defiance sets into motion a chain of events that culminates in Iblis's cosmic exile. It's a moment that carves his path distinctly separate from divine favor, propelling him into a role that is often misunderstood. Iblis, in his newfound position, takes on the mantle of tempter, a role that he embodies with a unique approach. Unlike the traditional perception of a forceful evil entity, Iblis operates on the principle of invitation rather than coercion. He tempts, he suggests, but he does not force. It's a subtle yet powerful method, likened to a siren call that beckon with the allure of the forbidden.

Accompanying Iblis in his mission are the Shaytans, beings often considered the lesser devils in the hierarchy of malevolent forces. These entities are akin to agents of temptation, carrying out Iblis' grand plan of leading humans astray. They work in the shadows of human consciousness, presenting distractions and moral dilemmas, much like incessant whispers that sway judgment and cloud moral clarity. The Shaytans' role is integral to Iblis' overarching objective, each playing their part in the grand design of testing human virtue and resolve.

In this context, Iblis emerges as a figure embodying more than mere rebellion. He represents a nuanced aspect of the human spiritual journey, symbolizing the eternal struggle between divine command and personal will. His story is not just one of fall and retribution, but also serves as a mirror to the complexities of moral choice and the ever-present nature of temptation in the human experience. As such, Iblis stands as a pivotal figure in Islamic theology, a catalyst for contemplation and understanding of the deeper aspects of faith and morality.

EASTERN ANALOGOUS FIGURES: FROM MARA TO ASURAS

As we traverse the diverse landscape of global mythology and religious belief systems, we encounter figures that, while distinct in their cultural contexts, resonate with familiar aspects of the figure known as Satan in Western traditions. These entities, from Buddhism and Hinduism, provide a rich and varied understanding of temptation, ambition, and spiritual resistance.

Mara: Buddhism's Master of Illusion and Temptation

In the serene and introspective world of Buddhism, we meet Mara, often considered the closest equivalent to a tempter or adversary. Mara's role in Buddhist lore is pivotal, particularly in the story of the Buddha's journey to enlightenment. Picture the scene: the Buddha, known as Siddhartha Gautama before his enlightenment, sits beneath the Bodhi tree, on the verge of uncovering the profound truths of existence. At this critical juncture, Mara appears, determined to disrupt this moment of cosmic significance.

Mara's tactics are a masterclass in distraction and temptation. He conjures visions of vast kingdoms, immense power, and seductive pleasures, each offering designed to sway Siddhartha from his meditative quest. It's akin to standing at the threshold of a monumental discovery, only to be besieged by alluring but ultimately hollow promises. Yet, Siddhartha's resolve is unwavering. In a defining act of spiritual defiance, he reaches out and touches the earth. This gesture is both a grounding act and a call for the Earth itself to bear witness to his right to seek and attain enlightenment. Faced with this unshakeable resolve, Mara is left with no option but to vanish, his efforts to derail Siddhartha's enlightenment rendered futile.

The Asuras: Hinduism's Ambitious and Jealous Deities

Venturing into the colorful and multifaceted pantheon of Hinduism, we encounter the Asuras. Originating as celestial beings, the Asuras' narrative takes a turn due to their excessive indulgence in pride and ego. They embody the darker aspects of ambition and rivalry, driven by a relentless thirst for power and dominion.

The Asuras are complex figures, embodying both nobility and baser instincts. They are powerful and charismatic, often depicted as mighty warriors and accomplished beings. However, their narratives are marred by their tendency to let jealousy and ambition guide their actions. In many tales, they find themselves in opposition to the Devas, the gods of the Hindu pantheon, resulting in epic battles and cosmic confrontations.

These celestial rebels share similarities with the concept of Satan as a fallen being. However, unlike the singular entity of Satan, the Asuras represent a collective, each with their unique stories and traits. Their actions often disrupt the cosmic order, leading to divine interventions and legendary battles. They are akin to those acquaintances who, despite their charisma and allure, bring chaos and drama, turning every interaction into a memorable but potentially troubling saga.

The Asuras' narrative is a cautionary tale about the perils of unchecked ego and ambition. Their downfall serves as a reminder of the delicate balance between power and humility, ambition and wisdom. In Hindu mythology, they continue to play a significant role, symbolizing the eternal struggle between good and evil, order and chaos, humility and pride.

Exploring these Eastern counterparts to Satan – Mara and the Asuras – enriches our understanding of the universal themes of temptation, ambition, and spiritual struggle. They offer a broader perspective on the archetypal battle between light and dark forces, a theme that resonates across cultures and belief systems. Mara and the Asuras, in their respective narratives, illustrate the myriad ways in which beings grapple with desire, power, and the pursuit of enlightenment, echoing the complexities and challenges inherent in the human spiritual journey.

A Grand Tour, A Cosmic Ensemble

That's actually quite remarkable, don't you agree? The profound demonstration of stubbornness by Islam's Iblis has revealed to us the astonishing heights to which this trait can reach, while also acknowledging the potential involvement of the Shaytans in any impulses you may experience that do not reflect holiness. In addition, we have also embarked on a brief journey through the rich traditions of the East, encountered various mischievous characters, and triumphed over a couple of formidable cosmic adversaries.

Each tradition paints its leading malevolent figure with unique strokes, yet they all capture some essence of what we've come to recognize in Satan—a complexity that defies simple evil, a rebellion that questions cosmic authority, and a story that's far too engaging to be confined to a single spiritual tradition.

The history doesn't stop there.

During the Medieval and Renaissance periods, it was common for painters to be fixated on capturing ethereal glows, cherubs were more secure in their employment than feudal lords, and depictions of Satan were, to put it mildly, exceptionally imaginative. Imagine the serene experience of leisurely strolling through the softly illuminated corridors of a majestic castle from the 16th century. You're more likely to find a painting of Satan on the wall than you are to get good Wi-Fi. Not that they had Wi-Fi, but you get the idea.

MEDIEVAL PORTRAYALS

In the medieval era, art and literature held a much broader significance and purpose than mere entertainment or aesthetic enjoyment. They were potent tools of moral instruction, deeply intertwined with the prevailing religious and ethical consciousness of the time. This period witnessed the emergence of some of the most vivid and symbolically charged portrayals of Satan, a figure who was depicted not merely as a conventional villain but as a manifestation of profound spiritual and moral conflict.

The depiction of Satan during these times was far from mundane. He was often presented as a beastly entity, amalgamating features of various animals that were imbued with negative connotations. Commonly, Satan bore a striking resemblance to goats and snakes, creatures that elicited a sense of unease or fear. This choice of representation was not arbitrary. The medieval mind was steeped in a culture where every image, symbol, and motif carried significant meaning, often serving as a visual sermon about virtue and vice.

It's my observation, this is where the spirit of Satan got slightly mingled with the Greek God Pan, which further distracted from Satan's actual form.

Symbolism in Satan's Portrayal

The frequent depiction of Satan with goat-like features was a deliberate choice, rich in symbolic meaning. In Christian iconography, the goat was often associated with lust, debauchery, and unrestrained carnal instincts. This linkage can be traced back to ancient pagan traditions where goats were symbols of fertility and lascivious behavior. By portraying Satan with the characteristics of a goat, artists and storytellers were not merely aiming to invoke fear but to convey a deeper moral message about the dangers of unchecked desire and the moral degradation it could lead to. I feel this was also an attempt to connect Satan with the Roman god Pan.

Similarly, the incorporation of serpentine elements in depictions of Satan drew upon the long-standing association of snakes with deceit and treachery. This symbolism harks back to the Biblical narrative of the Garden of Eden, where the serpent plays a pivotal role in the fall of man. The snake's image, therefore, became a potent reminder of Satan's role as the deceiver, the one who lures humans away from divine truth and into the perils of sin. Unfortunately, this also forms many people's aversions of snakes today. Snakes are actually lovely creatures, worthy of respect. In that way, I figure Satan is also worth of our respect.

Art and Literature as Moral Guides

In medieval society, art and literature served as visual and narrative guides to understanding complex theological and moral concepts. The portrayal of Satan was not merely about instilling fear; it was a part of a larger didactic strategy. These depictions were akin to moral compasses, guiding the faithful in recognizing and resisting the many faces of evil as represented by Satan.

The majority of the population in the medieval period was illiterate. Visual representations in art and dramatized stories in literature were crucial in educating the masses about the teachings of Christianity, including the nature of sin and the importance of moral vigilance.

Allegorical storytelling was a staple in medieval literature, where characters and narratives were imbued with multiple layers of meaning. Satan, in these allegories, was often a central figure, embodying the spiritual dangers that Christians were urged to guard against.

The way Satan was portrayed also reflected the prevailing cultural and social attitudes of the time. The fears, anxieties, and moral preoccupations of medieval society found expression in these artistic renditions, making Satan a figure that encapsulated the zeitgeist of the era.

The depiction of Satan in medieval art and literature was a complex and multifaceted phenomenon. It was an embodiment of the era's moral and spiritual concerns, rendered in forms that were both terrifying and instructive. These portrayals served as vivid reminders of the path of virtue and the pitfalls of vice, illustrating the eternal struggle between good and evil. In understanding these representations, one gains insight not only into the medieval mindset but also into the enduring power of symbols and narratives in shaping our understanding of moral and spiritual truths.

RENAISSANCE SATAN: THE SUAVE, SOPHISTICATED SEDUCER

As we journey through the annals of history to the Renaissance, a period marked by a resurgence in cultural, artistic, and intellectual vigor, we witness a fascinating evolution in the depiction of Satan. This era, known for its groundbreaking advancements in the arts and humanities, saw the transformation of Satan from a purely monstrous entity to a figure of complexity and charisma. The Renaissance, with its flourishing art scene and burgeoning intellectual discourse, provided the perfect crucible for this metamorphosis.

In the medieval period, Satan was predominantly depicted as a beastly, fear-inducing creature. However, the Renaissance brought about a significant shift. Artists and writers started to portray Satan as a more humanized figure, blending eloquence and charm with his traditionally malevolent attributes. This change in representation wasn't just aesthetic but deeply symbolic, reflecting the era's growing interest in human psychology and the complexities of moral and spiritual themes.

A quintessential example of Satan's transformed portrayal can be found in John Milton's epic poem, "Paradise Lost." Here, Satan is not just a fallen angel; he is a tragic, multifaceted character who articulates his rebellion against divine authority with persuasive eloquence. Milton's Satan is charismatic, complex, and in many ways, profoundly human.

He expresses emotions, reasons out his defiance, and, in doing so, becomes a character that readers can relate to, even empathize with. This portrayal was groundbreaking, as it invited readers to explore the nuanced dynamics of good and evil, freedom and subjugation, rebellion and obedience. (More on this in the next section.)

In the visual arts, the Renaissance artists began to depict Satan in a more human-like form. While the traditional representations of beasts and demons persisted, they increasingly took on subsidiary roles, orbiting around a central figure of Satan, who was now eerily relatable. These depictions often portrayed Satan as a figure embodying both beauty and moral ambiguity, challenging viewers to confront their perceptions of evil and temptation.

The Nuanced Terror of the Renaissance Satan

The humanization of Satan in Renaissance art and literature did not diminish his role as an embodiment of evil. Instead, it rendered him even more disturbing. The idea of a clever, charming Satan, one who could reason and persuade, presented a more complex and insidious type of villainy. It suggested a form of evil that was not just external and otherworldly, but one that could reside within the human psyche, capable of manipulation and deceit.

This shift in Satan's portrayal mirrored broader societal changes during the Renaissance. As humanism took root, and there was a greater focus on individual human experience and self-expression, the exploration of complex characters like Satan resonated with the intellectual and artistic climate of the time. It reflected a deepening interest in the inner workings of the human mind and the moral dilemmas faced by individuals.

In this era, Satan became a symbol for the broader moral and philosophical conflicts of humankind. His character invited contemplation on free will, the nature of rebellion against perceived tyranny, and the blurred lines between good and evil. This more sophisticated and humanized Satan was not just a character in stories and paintings; he was a conceptual tool for exploring the depths of moral philosophy and theological debate.

The Renaissance, with its profound impact on culture and thought, redefined the figure of Satan, transforming him from a straightforward embodiment of evil into a symbol of moral complexity and psychological depth. This period, renowned for its celebration of human potential and intellectual exploration, thus contributed significantly to the evolution of Satan as a character – one that continues to fascinate, terrify, and provoke thought in equal measure. The Renaissance Satan, both charismatic and cunning, stands as a testament to the era's lasting influence on how we interpret and depict the fundamental narratives of good and evil.

THE SHIFT IN PERSPECTIVE: OR HOW SATAN BECAME AN ANTI-HERO

The transition from the medieval to the Renaissance portrayals of Satan indicates a shift in human thought. Medieval Satan was all about embodying the terror of the unknown and the incomprehensible aspects of evil. Come Renaissance, and Satan starts to mirror our own complexities. Maybe society realized that evil isn't just an external force, but something that lurks within us all. A caution, perhaps, that the most dangerous demons are those that can charm us, seduce us, and make us question our most fundamental beliefs.

Why does this matter today, in a world where Satan often gets reduced to a cartoon character with a pitchfork? Because these rich historical perspectives offer us a mirror to our collective psyche. They show us how our understanding of good and evil, right and wrong, has evolved. And it's not just an academic exercise; these shifts in portrayal affected how people practiced magik, how they perceived the celestial balance, and how they interacted with energies that were once considered purely diabolical.

So, the next time you see a goat, don't just think about cheese. Remember, you're looking at an animal that was once the face of pure evil to an entire generation. And the next time you read an old book or study a painting, think about the layers of meaning, the centuries of human fear, aspiration, and understanding that are brushed into those strokes or woven into those words. It's more than art; it's the chronicle of humanity's ever-evolving relationship with the spiritual world.

The landscape of organizations that purport to worship Satan is as diverse as it is complex. However, it's crucial to note that many of these groups differ significantly in philosophy, practices, and the interpretation of what 'Satan' symbolizes. One of the most prominent and widely recognized among these is the Church of Satan. This book wouldn't be complete unless I mentioned these organizations. And more than one or two persist in the habit of mixed Satan with Lucifer, two distinct beings.

THE CHURCH OF SATAN

Founded in 1966 by Anton Szandor LaVey, the Church of Satan emerged as a formal organization dedicated to the philosophy now known as LaVeyan Satanism. This organization does not worship Satan as a deity, but views Satan as a symbol of certain human traits.

In LaVeyan Satanism, Satan is symbolized as an archetype of pride, liberty, and individualism. It's a representation of embracing one's true nature without guilt and living according to one's own standards.

Rituals in the Church of Satan are used as psychodramatic ceremonies to express personal needs or resolve emotional burdens. They are not perceived as supernatural occurrences, but as a form of emotional catharsis.

The Church of Satan promotes a set of ethics focused on self-preservation, personal responsibility, and merit. It advocates for the pursuit of personal desires as long as it does not harm others unjustly.

The Church of Satan, since its inception, has attracted significant attention and controversy. It has often been misunderstood and misrepresented by popular media and those outside the organization. Contrary to popular belief, the Church of Satan does not promote evil, cruelty, or theistic devil worship. Its philosophy is deeply rooted in secular and humanistic ideals.

OTHER SATANIC ORGANIZATIONS

Beyond the Church of Satan, there are numerous other groups and organizations with varying beliefs and practices that identify with Satanism. These include:

1. The Satanic Temple: A separate entity from the Church of Satan, known for its political activism and efforts to promote separation of church and state.

2. Theistic Satanism: Unlike LaVeyan Satanism, theistic Satanists do believe in Satan as a deity or supernatural being. However, their beliefs and practices vary widely.

3. Independent Satanic Groups: There are numerous smaller, independent groups and individuals who identify with Satanism or the occult in various ways, each with their own unique interpretation and practice.

As you can see, the spectrum of organizations that identify with Satanism is broad, with the Church of Satan being one of the most prominent and influential. It's important to approach these organizations with a nuanced understanding, recognizing the diversity in beliefs and practices within the umbrella of Satanism. The Church of Satan, in particular, stands as a testament to a non-theistic, symbolic interpretation of Satan, advocating for philosophical and ethical principles that challenge conventional religious and moral paradigms.

Now, I'm going to look at how most people view Satan - the Satan of popular culture, literature and modern media.

SATAN IN POPULAR CULTURE

In 1667, a pivotal moment in literary history was marked by the publication of John Milton's 'Paradise Lost,' a work that dramatically altered the traditional portrayal of Satan. In this epic poem, Satan is depicted not merely as a sinister antagonist, but as a complex and tragic hero. This representation was a significant departure from earlier portrayals, where Satan was often relegated to the role of a tempter lurking in the shadows. Milton's Satan, with his profound and eloquent monologues, brought a depth to the character that was previously unseen. His famous declaration, "Better to reign in Hell than serve in Heaven," encapsulates a newfound defiance and autonomy, positioning him as a figure of substantial agency and conflicted nobility.

Milton's reimagining of Satan had a profound impact on both literature and popular perception. This transformation could be likened to the way Charlotte Brontë revolutionized the archetype of the brooding male protagonist in romantic literature. Satan, under Milton's pen, became a character with whom audiences found an unexpected resonance. The complexity of his character allowed for a multifaceted interpretation, turning the once straightforward embodiment of evil into a figure capable of eliciting a degree of sympathy and contemplation.

As we leap forward into the age of modern cinema, the evolution of Satan's portrayal continued. The film industry, with its penchant for dramatic and visually stunning narratives, has offered various interpretations of this iconic figure. The transition from the ominous and foreboding presence in 'The Omen' to more nuanced, or even comedic, portrayals in films like 'Bedazzled,' demonstrates the versatility with which Satan has been depicted in popular culture.

'The Exorcist,' a landmark in horror cinema, is another significant milestone in the portrayal of Satan. The movie transcended the boundaries of entertainment, becoming a cultural phenomenon that profoundly impacted its audience. It sparked a widespread fascination with the supernatural and the demonic, leading many to seek spiritual refuge and purification. The portrayal of demonic possession in 'The Exorcist' was so impactful that it left an indelible mark on the collective psyche, reinforcing the terrifying power and presence of Satan in the popular imagination.

In more recent times, the character of Satan has been explored in various forms of media, including television. The show 'Lucifer,' for example, presents a version of Satan who is charming, urbane, and engaged in crime-solving - a far cry from the traditional image of the malevolent overlord. This interpretation, while unorthodox, adds layers of complexity to Satan's character, portraying him as multifaceted and capable of engaging in human affairs in ways that are intriguing and surprisingly relatable.

From Milton's profound literary portrayal to the diverse renditions in modern media, the character of Satan has undergone a remarkable evolution. This journey from feared antagonist to a character of deep complexity and varied interpretation underscores the enduring fascination and narrative potential that Satan holds in the cultural and artistic imagination.

SATANIC PANICS: THE HYPE TRAIN

In the 1980s, a cultural phenomenon swept across much of the United States and some other Western countries, known as the Satanic Panic. This period was marked by a growing fear of Satanism and occult practices infiltrating mainstream society, fears that were often unfounded but deeply impactful, nonetheless. It was a time characterized by a collective apprehension surrounding various forms of entertainment and community institutions, perceived as potential vessels for malevolent forces. This was mostly pushed by the super religious types in the US, centered around some southern states. Small, but very vocal groups.

It was almost as if society suddenly regressed to the 1600s. It was aggravating to someone like myself, all this finger pointing and running panic. Thing is, plenty of politicians took advantage of the gullible, and ran for office, which just inflamed the issue.

Dungeons & Dragons and Rock Music

Popular games like Dungeons & Dragons, along with certain genres of rock music, found themselves at the center of controversy in the US. Dungeons & Dragons, a fantasy role-playing game rich in imagination and storytelling, was accused of leading young people into occult practices. Critics of the game asserted that its intricate world-building and use of magikal elements could somehow entice players into real-world occultism. Similarly, rock music, particularly heavy metal, faced allegations of containing subliminal satanic messages. Lyrics and imagery often associated with rebellion and anti-establishment themes were interpreted as endorsements of Satanism.

The religious types would say that if you played a record album (on vinyl) backwards it'd recite some nefarious prayer to Satan. All it actually did was screw up the turntable's stylus and the record itself.

The 'Harry Potter' Controversy

The release of the 'Harry Potter' series in the late 1990s reignited some of these fears. The books, which quickly became a global phenomenon, were criticized by some groups who believed that their portrayal of witchcraft and wizardry could lead young readers into exploring the occult. Despite the series' focus on themes of friendship, courage, and moral choices, the mere presence of magikal elements was enough to cause alarm among those who saw it as a gateway to darker practices.

Daycare Accusations

One of the more disturbing aspects of the Satanic Panic was its impact on daycare centers. Across America, a series of high-profile cases arose where daycare staff were accused of engaging in satanic rituals and abuse. These allegations, often based on dubious evidence and the unreliable testimony of young children, led to a wave of hysteria. Innocent people found themselves embroiled in legal battles, their lives upended by the mere accusation of involvement in Satanism. The frenzy around these cases reflected a broader fear of moral decay and the potential corruption of innocence. More on this in a bit.

The Societal Impact

The Satanic Panic was more than a transient cultural oddity; it was indicative of deeper societal anxieties. It revealed underlying fears about the influence of media on young minds, the erosion of traditional values, and the perceived threats to the social order. The panic was less about the actual threat of Satanism and more about a society grappling with rapid cultural changes and looking for a scapegoat to explain the unexplainable or to rationalize the irrational.

Reflection

Looking back at the Satanic Panic from a contemporary perspective, it's clear that the fears and accusations were largely unfounded. However, the phenomenon left a lasting impact on how occult practices are perceived in popular culture. It serves as a reminder of the power of mass hysteria and the importance of critical thinking and evidence-based investigation. The Satanic Panic, in its essence, was a manifestation of the age-old conflict between fear of the unknown and the pursuit of rational understanding.

DAYCARE DRAMA: WHEN SATAN VISITED PRESCHOOL

You might be wondering, "Daycares? Really?" Oh yes, yes, indeed. The stage for the most infamous chapter of the Satanic Panic was not some eerie, secluded mansion; it was the neighborhood daycare centers, where children were supposed to be safe. This was no laughing matter. Suddenly, your kid's drawings of pentagrams or odd mentions of rituals had parents racing to pick them up faster than you could say, "Rubber duckie, you're the one."

McMartin Preschool: Ground Zero for the Panic

The epicenter of this hysteria was the McMartin Preschool in Manhattan Beach, California. The saga began when a mother accused a staff member of molestation, but it spiraled into full-blown accusations of Satanic rituals. There were allegations of underground tunnels, animal sacrifices, and children being flown on private planes to engage in dark ceremonies. Never mind that none of this was substantiated; the witch hunt—quite literally—had begun.

Investigations were carried out, but not in the way you'd imagine. There was suggestive questioning, and I don't mean that in a sly, nudge-nudge, wink-wink way. Interviewers would ask leading questions that encouraged children to disclose satanic abuse, effectively implanting memories. Imagine being so young and impressionable, and adults are telling you that you've been a part of a sinister magik ritual. Before you know it, everyone's sipping that panic-induced Kool-Aid.

So, there were trials, right? Oh, you bet. The McMartin Preschool trial was one of the longest and most expensive criminal trials in American history. In the end, no convictions were made, but lives were irreparably damaged. Careers were ruined, reputations tarnished, and all over allegations that were never proven.

The Aftermath: When the Dust Settled

You might say, "Okay, the '80s are long gone. Why should I care?" Here's why: the Satanic Panic serves as a cautionary tale of how collective fear can distort reality. It underscores the enormous responsibility wielded by practitioners of magik, occult scholars, and even average people dabbling in spiritual arts. The way you channel energies and engage with entities not only has an effect on you but can resonate throughout society, especially when society is already on the brink of its own irrational fears.

If you're involved in magik, you must remember that it's not just about lighting candles and chanting in forgotten languages. It's about understanding that the spiritual is also political and social. You could be the most ethical and enlightened person, but if society misunderstands or misrepresents what you do, you can get swept up in a wave of fear and ignorance.

So, as you trace your sigils and prepare your sacred space, remember this chapter from the not-so-distant past. It stands as a reminder that the practice of magik isn't just a personal journey but one that weaves through the tapestry of collective human experience. Whether you're summoning a daemon or invoking a goddess, be mindful of the energies you engage with. Your actions, in a hyper-connected, hyper-sensitive world, could be the difference between fostering understanding or fueling another round of destructive, baseless panic. Moving on!

THE CROSSOVER EPISODES

Now, think about this. How many literary and cinematic figures have had the honor of appearing in religious texts, classic literature, blockbuster movies, and even moral panics? Very few. Satan is that rare character who's transcended his original 'casting' to play roles in a myriad of human dramas, comedies, and thrillers. I thought Lucifer got a lot of press. Oh no.

Satan is more than a figure of evil or rebellion; he's a symbol, a warning, a challenge, and, dare I say it, an inspiration for many stories that question the very nature of good and evil, right and wrong, sin and redemption. When Dante wrote 'Inferno,' he put Satan at the center of Hell, but he also made us question who really deserves to be there.

We've seen how Satan's been reimagined, rebranded, and rebooted more times than Spider-Man. Through each lens—literary, cinematic, or sensational—he offers a different face, and not always one you'd expect.

Satan keeps evolving, and that, my friends, is what makes him such a compelling character to study and understand, especially when we consider his role in the esoteric arts of magik. Because trust me, this isn't the last act, and the next scene is already set for some spellbinding drama. Are you not entertained? Good, because the show's just getting started.

POPULAR NICKNAMES FOR SATAN

Before I get into the aspects of Satan, I thought I'd generate a short list of popular nicknames for His Darkness. Then I wound up with a long, long list. 40 to be exact. I only have a few nicknames myself. There's some there I'd not heard of, and some I knew about, but this is probably not even a complete list. I even had one father of a young woman I was dating actually call me the "Anti Christ." Oh, then a neighbor lady called me "quite the macabre boy", which I figured is actually a badge of honor.

However, I'm sure there are some of ya'll who will know of a few more Satanic nicknames and will email me about it.

1. Aduwallah
2. Adversary
3. Al-Shaytaan
4. Antichrist
5. archfiend
6. Ash-Shaytan

7. Azazel
8. Beast
9. Beelzebub
10. bogey (archaic)
11. cosmocrat
12. deceiver
13. deuce
14. Devil
15. El diablo
16. Diabolus
17. dickens
18. Dragon
19. Evil One
20. Father of Lies
21. Gog
22. Iblis
23. Jack Ketch
24. lord of the flies
25. Lucifer
26. Mephistopheles
27. Old Gentleman
28. Old Hairy
29. Old Harry
30. Old Nick
31. Old One
32. Old Scratch
33. Old Serpent

34. Prince of Darkness

35. Prince of Demons

36. Prince of Evil

37. Sam Scratch

38. Satan

39. shaitan

40. Son of the Dawn

Well, okay. Wow. Yeah. Okay - I figure it's about time to get to the nugget of this book and let's get to the magik!

CHAPTER 2

ASPECTS OF SATAN

Well, okay - let's first look at the aspects we'll be using. Due to needing to limit the pages in this book, I'm not actually going to explore every single aspect that Satan possesses. Instead, I'm going to match specific magik rituals to a specific aspect. There will be, undoubtedly, an aspect I skipped which you may wish to explore. Such as a feminine aspect, closer to Lilith than any other feminine spirit. Use what resonates with you and your goals. Some people tend to use only the Egregore aspect, and that's fine, but there are several others with really nice energy in ritual. Might think of Satan as a brand of energy, like a brand of fine Scotch whiskey. You will prefer one over another.

My ultimate goal is to lead people towards enlightenment, so I start with that aspect.

TRANSFORMATION AND ENLIGHTENMENT

Satan's role as a bringer of enlightenment is a complex and deeply layered aspect that resonates with various mythological and philosophical narratives, most notably with the tale of Prometheus, who defied the gods to bring fire to humanity. In this context, Satan represents not just rebellion, but the quest for knowledge and truth, often of a kind that is shrouded in secrecy or deemed forbidden by societal norms and traditional dogmas.

This aspect of Satan challenges the practitioner to venture beyond the surface of conventional wisdom to seek truths that lie hidden beneath layers of prohibition and caution. It's a call to explore the uncharted territories of knowledge, to question what has been accepted without scrutiny, and to dare to think and understand beyond the boundaries set by orthodox belief systems. Engaging with this aspect of Satan in magikal practices involves a deep commitment to learning, understanding, and, most importantly, questioning.

The pursuit of this forbidden knowledge often leads to significant personal transformation. It's akin to opening a Pandora's box of wisdom where each piece of knowledge challenges and reshapes one's understanding of the world. This process can be both exhilarating and daunting, as it often requires the individual to reconstruct their worldview, to let go of long-held beliefs, and to embrace new, sometimes radical, ideas. This transformative power of knowledge is at the heart of Satan's role as an enlightener.

In a broader sense, this pursuit of enlightenment is not just about gaining information or learning new things. It's about achieving a deeper level of consciousness and understanding.

It's a spiritual journey that involves the illumination of the mind and soul. By engaging with this aspect of Satan, one is not merely seeking to become more knowledgeable but is striving to achieve a higher state of being, a more profound connection with the universe, and a more intimate understanding of the self.

This enlightenment often comes with its own set of challenges and responsibilities. Knowledge, especially of the kind considered forbidden or profound, carries with it a weight of responsibility. It demands ethical considerations and introspection about how this knowledge is used and for what purpose. Engaging with Satan in the quest for enlightenment thus involves not only the pursuit of knowledge but also the cultivation of wisdom – the ability to use knowledge with discernment and ethical consideration.

Satan's role as a bringer of enlightenment in the world of magik and occult is rich with symbolic and practical significance. It represents a fearless journey into the depths of forbidden knowledge, a transformative process of personal evolution, and a profound quest for spiritual understanding. This pursuit is as challenging as it is rewarding, requiring practitioners to constantly balance their quest for knowledge with a sense of moral and ethical responsibility.

MATERIAL MASTERY AND EARTHLY POWER

This is quite a popular aspect.

Satan is often connected to the accumulation of material wealth and the exercise of earthly power in many occult practices. This aspect presents Satan as a figure symbolizing the mastery of the physical realm and the ability to turn desires into tangible manifestations. The concept being discussed here explores the deep and intricate connection between the spiritual and the material aspects, highlighting how the spiritual realm can be utilized as a means to impact and mold the physical world.

Engaging with Satan in this context is to tap into an ancient force that speaks to the very core of human ambition – the desire to acquire, to possess, and to exercise dominion over one's surroundings. It's a magikal endeavor that transcends mere materialism; it's about harnessing the energies of the universe to bring about real-world changes. This aspect of Satan encourages practitioners to boldly claim their space in the world, to assert their will, and to actively shape their destiny.

This quest for material wealth and power is often viewed through a lens of pragmatism and realism. It acknowledges the importance of material resources in achieving comfort, stability, and influence in the physical world. Engaging with this aspect of Satan is not merely about greed or the lust for riches; it's about understanding and utilizing the laws of nature and the universe to create abundance and prosperity. It's an acknowledgment that while spiritual enlightenment is paramount, material resources are crucial in providing the foundation upon which one can build a fulfilling life.

However, this pursuit is not without its challenges and complexities. It requires a deep understanding of one's true desires and the implications of manifesting them. It demands introspection and self-awareness to ensure that the quest for material gain does not overshadow one's spiritual growth or ethical values. You must navigate this path with a sense of responsibility and wisdom, using their material gains not for selfish ends but as tools for personal development, for helping others, and for contributing positively to the world.

Moreover, invoking Satan for material wealth and power calls for a balanced approach. It involves aligning one's personal energies with the energies of abundance and prosperity, while remaining grounded in spiritual truth. This balance ensures that the pursuit of material wealth does not lead to spiritual bankruptcy but instead contributes to a well-rounded, fulfilling life experience.

In essence, the association of Satan with material wealth and earthly power in magik and occult practices is a multifaceted concept. It is about the empowerment to change one's life circumstances, the ability to bring about tangible results through spiritual means, and the wisdom to use material resources in a way that enhances rather than detracts from one's spiritual and ethical integrity.

This material mastery also can be used to control others. In a later chapter, I'll go in depth on this aspect and how it can be used to exert control over others. Do be warned, this will violate the free will of the targets. However, Satan doesn't care so much for people easily led by others.

SEXUALITY AND LIBERATION:

This is another popular use of Satan's powers. I know I have used his powers in this regard once I'd learned my lessons about compelling someone to come to me. After that, I wield this power with restraint.

His association with sexual energy and the breaking of sexual taboos is a theme that resonates with profound depth and complexity. This aspect of Satan is not merely about indulgence or hedonism; it's a profound embrace of the acceptance of natural desires, a call to challenge and transcend societal norms that have long constrained human sexuality.

This representation of Satan as an emblem of sexual liberation and power delves into the very core of human nature. It acknowledges sexuality as a fundamental and potent force in human existence, a source of creative energy, personal empowerment, and transformation. Invoking Satan in this context is to engage with the primal aspects of one's being, to explore and embrace one's sexual identity without shame or guilt. It's an invitation to step out of the shadows of repression and into the light of self-acceptance and expression.

The breaking of sexual taboos, under Satan's aegis, goes beyond mere defiance of societal norms. It's an act of liberation from the chains of dogma, stigma, and misinformation that have historically surrounded human sexuality. This aspect encourages individuals to question and dismantle the outdated and often harmful beliefs that have been imposed upon them, be it by culture, religion, or societal expectations. It's about reclaiming one's right to pleasure, intimacy, and sexual expression in ways that are healthy, consensual, and affirming.

Engaging with this aspect of Satan in magikal practices often involves rituals and spells that not only aim to enhance sexual attraction and prowess but also to heal sexual traumas, to empower one's sexual identity, and to foster deeper, more meaningful connections with partners. It's about using sexual energy not just for physical gratification but as a tool for spiritual growth and personal empowerment. The rituals I list are simple examples, and you can craft your own petition using the ritual templates I provide.

Moreover, this aspect challenges magicians to confront and integrate their shadow selves. In Jungian psychology, the shadow self is the part of us that we repress or deny, often including sexual aspects of our personality. By embracing this aspect of Satan, one is encouraged to explore and integrate these repressed parts, leading to a more holistic understanding of oneself.

However, this journey is not without its challenges. It requires a deep sense of self-awareness, responsibility, and ethical consideration. It demands that practitioners navigate their sexual exploration with respect for themselves and others, always prioritizing consent and emotional well-being.

This aspect will also be summoned when we need to control others, when we need to influence someone's opinion of us to advance in business or in social or political situations. Along with all the ramifications attached to this type of magik.

SATAN THE EGREGORE

The concept of an egregore in occult and esoteric traditions refers to a collective thought-form or psychic entity, created and sustained by the beliefs, emotions, and energies of a group of people. It's an amalgamation of collective consciousness that takes on a life of its own, influenced by the intentions and perceptions of those who feed into it. In the context of Satan, the egregore aspect represents a powerful, autonomous force shaped by centuries of human belief, fear, reverence, and revulsion.

Over millennia, the figure of Satan has been the focus of intense emotions, from fear and hatred to veneration and fascination. These collective human energies have contributed to the creation of a potent egregore. This egregore of Satan is not just a symbol but an active psychic entity, influenced by the myriad ways in which humanity has perceived him. It's a manifestation that embodies the accumulated attributes, powers, and characteristics attributed to Satan over ages.

In this egregore form, Satan transcends individual identity, becoming a powerful archetype that exists independently of any single myth or tradition. This aspect is both shaped by and shapes the collective consciousness, acting as a mirror to humanity's deepest fears, desires, and shadows.

We'll be using this form in any magik associated with baneful magik, which is the best use of this aspect I can suggest. Some have said this is like having a tiger as a pet. I'm not sure about that analogy, but this form is quite powerful and unpredictable.

Balance of Light and Darkness

In magik, the concept of Satan, much like Lilith, is not defined by a simple duality of light and dark. Rather, it embodies a continuum, a gradation that stretches from one extreme to the other, akin to a spectrum of 256 shades of gray, reminiscent of the grayscale limits found in early digital imagery. This spectrum implies that no single aspect of Satan's energy is purely benevolent or malevolent; instead, each point along this continuum offers a different blend of qualities and potential applications in magik.

Modern digital images contain quite a bit more grayscale points than those early images. Think more like 4,000+ steps from white to black. Sure beats only 50 shades.

The gradation of light and darkness in Satan's energy is symbolic of the complexities and contradictions inherent in life and magik. In this spectrum, the lighter shades might represent the aspects traditionally associated with positive energies — healing, protection, or benevolent influence. In contrast, the darker shades might embody the energies often perceived as negative — such as those used in baneful magik or for exerting control. However, these distinctions are not rigid; the energies of Satan exist in a state of fluidity, allowing you to draw upon the necessary shade to suit your specific magikal needs and intentions.

This nuanced understanding of Satan's energy is particularly beneficial for practices like shadow work. Shadow work involves delving into the deeper, often unacknowledged parts of your psyche, confronting and integrating aspects of yourself that you might have suppressed or ignored. The spectrum of Satan's energy provides a rich resource for this introspective journey, offering the courage and insight necessary to navigate through the darker recesses of your soul and emerge with greater self-awareness and understanding.

Similarly, in the pursuit of transformation and enlightenment, the gradation of Satan's energy can be a guiding force. It encourages you to embrace change and growth, even when it involves traversing challenging or uncomfortable paths. This process is about evolving, gaining wisdom from each experience, whether it's bathed in light or shrouded in darkness.

By embracing the full spectrum of Satan's energy in your magikal practice, you adopt a holistic approach. You learn to appreciate and utilize both the light and dark aspects of your experiences, recognizing that each has its role to play in your spiritual and personal growth. This approach allows for a more profound and meaningful engagement with magik, where transformation and enlightenment are achieved through the integration and understanding of the entire range of life's experiences.

In essence, the balance of light and darkness in Satan's energy is not about choosing between good and evil. It's about acknowledging and working with the entire spectrum, understanding that every shade, every nuance, has its significance and purpose in the grand scheme of your magikal and spiritual journey.

BENEVOLENT PROTECTOR

Here's one aspect of Satan that often surprises many is his benevolent side, particularly in the areas of healing and protection magik. Contrary to popular belief, Satan, as a symbol and entity in magik, isn't solely associated with malevolence or destructive forces. Instead, there exists a compassionate dimension to his energy, which you can harness for healing and safeguarding purposes.

When you turn to Satan's energy for healing, you're tapping into a powerful source of renewal and restoration. This aspect of Satanic magik is about embracing your inner strength and resilience to overcome physical, emotional, or spiritual ailments. It involves channeling the energy to focus on the areas of your life or your being that need healing. The process can manifest in various forms, such as meditative practices where you focus on directing healing energy to yourself or others, or through rituals that symbolize and enact recovery and rejuvenation.

Similarly, the benevolent aspect of Satan can be invoked for protection. This facet of Satanic magik is about creating barriers against negative influences and energies. When you engage in protection work under this aspect, you're not only setting up defenses but also reinforcing your personal power and will against adversity. Protection rituals can involve creating physical representations of barriers, such as circles or sigils, and mentally charging them with the intent of safety and security. These practices are grounded in the belief that you have the power to shield yourself from harm, with Satan's energy acting as a bolstering force.

This benevolent aspect of Satan in magik offers a unique and powerful way to approach healing and protection. It challenges the conventional perceptions of Satanic magik, revealing a side that is nurturing, restorative, and defensive. By exploring and utilizing this aspect, you open yourself to a broader understanding of magik's potential and the multifaceted nature of Satanic energy.

Each of these aspects offers a different lens through which to understand and work with Satan in magikal practices. They reflect a complex and often paradoxical character, far removed from the simplistic embodiment of evil as often portrayed in mainstream narratives. Engaging with these different aspects can provide a deeper, more nuanced understanding of Satan's role in various spiritual and magikal systems.

As I present ritual for specific purposes, there will be specific sigils needed plus aspect specific summonings for the rituals. I encourage you to experiment, keeping a log or journal, when working with Satan. Take my suggested rituals and expand them, alter them for a specific purpose, and record the results. You may be surprised that you can so easily work with such a spirit as Satan, but always keep in mind that He's a very powerful spirit, and his personality has been shaped by history. He is slippery and will look for ways to deliver a desire in unexpected ways. Pay close attention to my precautions.

SATAN LOVES A GOOD LAUGH

In my book on Lilith, I recount the time I first used Satan in ritual. That first time did not work. Bad for me, I wanted it to work. Good for the young woman I targeted.

But years later, this sex slave ritual worked. Buoyed by this success, I immediately fired off another ritual. As I have previously written, the rituals ALL worked, and the first ritual didn't just stop when the second one started. No. I got myself in some trouble, especially since I'd ran the ritual many, many times.

I'm sure Satan laughed very loudly as I learned a valuable lesson. Don't muck with magik. It's real, and it works.

Before we get into the magik of this spirit, a few words of caution.

The Three L's: Laws, Legislation, and ... Satan

In this universe, or multiverse (for the more cosmically inclined among us), there are a few irrevocable laws. Gravity keeps us grounded, time remains linear-ish, and meddling with dark forces involves more legalities than you'd think. Even in matters of the infernal, we can't escape a bit of bureaucracy. I'm certain Satan has make copious notes of the human's habit of embellishing red tape and creating bureaucracies that only humans can create.

Witchcraft, as we've known it, has been shrouded with all sorts of legal hullabaloo throughout history. From the Witch Trials of Europe to modern-day legislation that somehow still finds a way to poke its nose into your incense-lit sanctuaries. So, even as you chant incantations and offer your libations, you should know the ins and outs of what you're allowed to do. A summoning gone wrong could spell more than just spiritual trouble—it could mean legal headaches, too.

But let's circle back. Don't want to scare you off just yet; we're only getting to the saucy parts.

The Morality Scale: Are You Good, Bad, or Chaotic Neutral?

Morality is a tricky subject, isn't it? It's more flexible than a yoga instructor on a caffeine high. Is working with Satan inherently bad, or could there be a beneficial side to it? The knee-jerk reaction is to slide it into the 'morally reprehensible' category, but isn't that a simplistic view?

Let me tell you a little story. When I was but a young magikal student, I was adamant about using my newfound knowledge for purely virtuous causes (No; I used my knowledge for purely selfish reasons.). Yes, I looked at healing, protection, money; you know the drill. But then, a fiery red-headed young woman, a student, I'll call her "Barbara," moved into the apartment next to me. I casually spotted her in a bikini by the pool later that month, because it stays bikini weather until mid-October in my home town. Mercy! I casually asked her to model for me, as I was a budding photographer. She said yes. Suddenly, I found myself tempted to explore the spicier side of the magikal spectrum. Did I do it? I won't kiss and tell. (Okay, this is one of those times I carefully used that sex ritual, and yes, it worked. I only exposed one half of a roll of film.) But it did force me to wrestle with my own moral compass. Is it alright to use magik to satisfy a hunger that won't go away? If we're talking in RPG terms, did it flip me from a Lawful Good to a Chaotic Neutral?

I spent all of fifteen minutes on this dilemma, then popped open another beer. (At this time, in the 1980s, drinking age was 18. And the beer was Shiner Bock.)

The Ethics of Intent: An Infernal Subjectivity

But let's not beat around the burning bush, so to speak. The crux of the matter often lies in intent. Are you seeking knowledge, empowerment, or perhaps vengeance? Ah, the sweet, nectar-like taste of vengeance. But remember, with great power comes—oh, you know the rest. The question here isn't just what you can do, but what you should do.

It's a conundrum as old as time—or at least as old as the first time someone realized they could get more than just milk from a cow. The ethical considerations of working with Satan are far-reaching and deeply personal. Just because you can make someone trip in front of their crush doesn't mean you should. Or should you? It's a zesty ethical pickle. I'm up for a good laugh. So is Satan.

The Satan Clause: Terms and Conditions Apply

You might think that partnering with Satan gives you a free pass to live out your most indulgent fantasies. But not so fast. Contracts with entities like Satan often come with strings attached—more like chains, really. Even if you've followed every legal guideline, crossed your "t"s and dotted your "i"s, it doesn't mean you've covered the moral or ethical grounds.

Think of it this way: you wouldn't sign a business contract without reading the fine print, right? Satan's contracts, verbal or otherwise, are no different. So, while you're flipping through your grimoires and double-checking your pentagrams, maybe throw in a quick skim of your local laws, just to make sure you're not inadvertently planning something that'll get you in a bind—both magikally and legally.

In the chapter on Pactmaking, I'll cover how to make sure the desire is delivered, with no "gotchas" on the part of Satan.

The Cosmic Balance: A Friendly Reminder

A warning: The universe has a quirky way of balancing things out. Call it karma, divine justice, or just poetic irony. When you dance with the Devil, make sure you know the steps, because trust me, he's got moves you've never even heard of.

So, moral of our story? Entering into any kind of pact with Satan isn't just a question of magik and spirituality. It's about legality and ethics, each as important and as complex as the other. You're not just dabbling in rites and rituals; you're dabbling in questions that philosophers, scholars, and yes, even lawyers, have pondered for eons.

Ah, the dance continues, the quill beckons, and the inkwell is far from dry. The chronicle of Satan is a tome written in fire and ash, in dreams and in harsh wakefulness. So take this lesson to heart. Before you take another step on this twisted path, consider the price, in both the corporeal and the ethereal. Because, let's be honest, no one wants to get burned.

But enough about the serious stuff! Loosen that tie, let down that hair, and crack those knuckles. There's more precautions you need to know about.

PRECAUTIONS

Summoning and petitioning Satan can become the spiritual equivalent of riding a roller coaster with no seatbelt while juggling flaming swords. And the roller coaster is on fire. The scaffolding is on fire. Hell, everything is on fire. The entire amusement park is on fire.

In short, it's not for the faint-hearted—or the under-prepared. Now, grab your wand or athame (that's a fancy ritual knife for the magikally uninitiated), because we're about to get into some serious stuff. And by serious, I mean the kind of stuff that makes your average love spell look like child's play. But first, a word of caution: with great power comes great—yeah, yeah, you get it.

But listen, it's absolutely true, especially in high magik. I'm serious. Read this chapter twice. Use a highlighter and just color in this whole section.

High magik is the grand opera of the magikal world. It involves intricate rituals, complex symbols, and, more often than not, some very heavy philosophical quandaries. While there are many paths in magik, they all lead to the summit of Mount Olympus or perhaps some other ethereal height where high magik reigns supreme. No shortcuts. If you think you can just snap your fingers and jump to the climax, man, you're gravely mistaken.

And speaking of being mistaken, let's bust a myth. High magik isn't just about the "high" or superior parts of yourself or the universe. It's about integrating both light and dark, understanding the balance between the two. A little like yin and yang, but with more chanting and less takeaway Chinese food.

Responsibility: You've Got the Whole World in Your Hands—Sort Of

This is where the responsibility part comes into play. Remember that feeling you had when you first realized you could tap into magik? It was like realizing you had superpowers, wasn't it? Imagine that sensation, but cranked up to eleven.

One story that comes to mind involves a friend—let's call him Tim. Tim was enchanted by high magik. He loved the ritualistic elegance, the symbolic richness, and the feeling of raw energy coursing through his veins. But he once skipped some crucial preparatory steps during a major invocation. The result? His cat started speaking in tongues, and his refrigerator... well, let's just say it's now a subject of a local urban legend. And that's what happens when you mess with forces that you haven't quite grasped yet.

In essence, practicing high magik is like being handed the nuclear launch codes of your own spiritual journey. Sure, you're curious about what that big red button does, but are you absolutely certain you should push it? Maybe you can, but should you? That's a big, loaded "should," my friend.

This is the fine line between hubris and wisdom. Wisdom whispers in your ear, "Hold on, hotshot. Maybe summoning a rain of frogs isn't what the drought-stricken landscape needs. Perhaps you should consult the Oracle—or, you know, a meteorologist."

The Soul's Curriculum: The Learning Never Stops

The Soul's Curriculum—a topic as expansive as the cosmos themselves. While you may think you're just dabbling in some fancy rituals with incense that smells like a woodland deity's armpit, what you're really doing is enrolling in a university as old as existence itself. But don't worry; there are no student loans in this school, although the textbooks (ancient grimoires, anyone?) might cost you an arm and a leg, metaphorically speaking, of course.

High magik isn't some one-off course you can cram for in a couple of sleepless nights with Red Bull by your side. No, sir, or madam, or however you identify. This is a labyrinthine journey without a definite end. Each day you're encountering new twists and turns, forks in the road where you'll need to decide whether to call upon Hermes for guidance or trust your own intuition. There's always another layer to peel, another dimension to explore, another spirit to consult. And just when you think you've reached a plateau, you realize it's just a rest stop, and there are more peaks to climb. Isn't that just like life, but with more pentagrams?

Your Soul, The Ultimate Exam

In most exams, you can peek over someone's shoulder or, these days, Google the answers. In the realm of conventional examinations, one might stealthily glance towards a neighboring classmate's scribbles for inspiration, or even resort to the modern practice of discreetly searching the internet for answers. But high magik? Man, it operates on an entirely different paradigm; it's an existential examination that is as an open book as they come, but the 'book' in question is none other than your very own soul. Moreover, the language in which this unique 'textbook' is composed is an esoteric dialect that is discernible solely to you.

Each syllable of every incantation you utter, each intricate line in the sigils you meticulously inscribe, each ceremonial chalice you raise towards the heavens in a room illuminated solely by the flickering light of candles—these are not just actions but profound questions aimed at plumbing the depths of your innermost being. The queries they pose are unambiguous but deeply complex: Are you fully aware of the intentions that guide your ritualistic actions? Have you contemplated the broad and intricate repercussions these acts might have on your spiritual trajectory?

Here, there is no generous grading curve to cushion your ego or rescue you from the jaws of failure. Your performance in this metaphysical assessment is dichotomous: you either excel by attaining perfect harmony between your actions and your spiritual aspirations, or you disastrously miss the mark. In the latter scenario, the consequences are not merely a failing grade or academic humiliation; rather, they may require you to undergo spiritual remediation. And that's a euphemistic way of putting it, because the stakes are infinitely higher. If you don't get it right, you risk triggering not just a personal setback but a perturbation in the cosmic equilibrium—a disruption in the sensitive web of energies and forces that hold the multiverse together. To put it simply, you could be the cause of a cosmic hiccup that reverberates across planes of existence.

Remember, Satan does not grade on a curve.

The Butterfly Effect: The Mystical Wi-Fi

We've all heard of the butterfly effect, right? A butterfly flaps its wings, and halfway across the world, someone spills their beer. Now, apply that to high magik. Your rituals, choices, and even thoughts create ripples in the pool of collective energy we're all splashing around in. Think of high magik as mystical Wi-Fi. Your practices are like data packets transmitted into the ether. Do it right, and you elevate the whole network's bandwidth; mess it up, and you're the reason everyone's streaming starts buffering at the most inconvenient times.

Let's bring Carl Jung into the party. He was quite the magikal guy, you know, with all that talk about archetypes and the collective unconscious. Well, your high magik rituals resonate through that same massive underground reservoir of shared symbols, dreams, and fears. When you invoke Aphrodite, you're not only dialing into your own love aspirations but also tapping into every love song ever written, every first kiss, every heartbreak. Your magik stirs the communal pot of human experience. No pressure, but you're the one seasoning the collective stew of subconscious drives and desires.

The Spiritual Influence: A Two-Way Street

High magik isn't just about affecting your immediate surroundings or personal goals. Whether you're summoning the West Wind for a change in luck or invoking an archangel for wisdom, your actions are akin to picking up a cosmic telephone and calling long-distance. Only, in this case, the call is received by, well, everyone and everything connected to the intricate tapestry of existence. Just remember, while you may be making the call, the universe always has the option of putting you on hold—or hanging up.

As you practice high magik, you might stumble upon entirely new realms of experience, ideas, or spirits hitherto unknown or misunderstood. It's akin to Christopher Columbus thinking he discovered a new route to India but ending up in an entirely different 'New World.' Except, you know, without the colonial implications. And every time you break new ground, you enrich not only your own magikal atlas but also expand the collective human understanding of what's possible, adding another star to our communal celestial navigation.

So, as you go deeper into the labyrinth of high magik, you'll find that you're not just a student but also a cartographer, an explorer, and—let's be honest—a bit of a cosmic daredevil. But with every invocation, every circle drawn, and every deity appeased, you're also a teacher, adding your own unique frequency to the cosmic tune we're all unconsciously humming.

And remember, in the realm of high magik, the bell never rings, and class is never dismissed. Your spiritual homework is never-ending, but so are the rewards.

The Subtlety of Balance: The Ultimate Juggling Act

Just like a tightrope walker, it takes skill and precision to manage your own energy and responsibility while engaging in high magik. Except this tightrope is made of spider silk and spans across the Grand Canyon. Yeah, it's delicate and risky, but oh, the view! If done correctly, with the necessary respect and due diligence, you're in for an eye-opening journey that will leave your spirit immeasurably enriched.

As you step onto the spider silk tightrope, you feel the weight of your energy and responsibility. Every step must be calculated, every movement deliberate. The Grand Canyon stretches out before you, a magnificent expanse of natural beauty that serves as a backdrop to your magical endeavor.

The delicacy of the spider silk reminds you of the fragility of the energies you are about to manipulate. One wrong move, one lapse in concentration, and the entire delicate balance could be disrupted. But the risk is worth it, for the reward is beyond measure.

With utmost respect for the forces at play, you begin your journey. Each step is a dance, a synchrony between your intention and the subtle energies around you. You feel the power of the canyon beneath your feet, the ancient wisdom embedded in its depths.

As you traverse the invisible path, you become attuned to the rhythm of the elements. The wind whispers secrets, carrying the echoes of ancient chants. The sun bathes you in its warm embrace, infusing you with vitality. The rocks, steeped in history, offer their stability and grounding energy.

You navigate the challenges that arise with grace and precision. Your focus is unwavering, your concentration unwavering. You harness the raw energy of the universe, channeling it through your being. The spider silk holds firm, a testament to your skill and mastery.

And then, as you reach the other side, a profound sense of awe washes over you. The view from this vantage point is breathtaking. The vastness of the Grand Canyon stretches out before you, a reminder of the limitless possibilities that exist within the realm of magic.

But it is not just the physical view that leaves you enriched. It is the journey itself, the experience of managing your energy and responsibility amidst the grandeur of high magik. You have been transformed, your spirit expanded and enlightened.

You carry this newfound wisdom with you as you step off the spider silk tightrope. The delicate and risky endeavor has rewarded you with a deeper understanding of the interconnectedness of all things. You are now equipped to navigate the realms of high magik with even greater skill and precision, forever enriched by the eye-opening journey across the Grand Canyon.

Tread Lightly but Carry a Big Stick

If magik is a garden, high magik is that exotic, carnivorous plant at the very center: intriguing, intoxicating, but handle with care. Always remember, it's not just about the razzle-dazzle of grandiose rituals or the adrenaline rush of wielding immense power. It's about the deep, resonating echo of responsibility that trails behind every incantation, every gesture, and every summoning circle you draw.

So as you stand at the precipice of this thrilling venture into high magik, don your ceremonial robes, light your candles, but above all, don your mantle of responsibility. It's the most crucial accessory you'll ever need.

Now, listen up a bit. You see, magik isn't just about drawing fancy sigils in the air while chanting verses that could make Shakespeare wish he were a magician. No, no, no! Practicing magik—especially high magik—is a high-stakes game. Imagine standing on a seesaw, balancing the weight of the cosmos on one side and your own sanity on the other. Sounds intense? You bet it is.

Now, before we all start looking like frightened rabbits, let's address the elephant in the room. Can practicing magik mess you up? The answer is a resounding yes, but only if you skip doing your homework. That's right, put down your athame and pay attention, because this is serious.

Spiritual Risks: How to Not Accidentally Summon a Cosmic Monster

Firstly, let's talk spiritual risks. Picture this: you're in your dimly lit sanctuary, feeling like the Merlin of the 21st century, and you begin a ritual. Candles flickering, incense swirling, you're feeling the energy. You mumble incantations, but oops—you lose focus, you think you've mispronounced some words, so you panic. Your panic manifests. Next thing you know, you've summoned something that makes Cthulhu look like a cute puppy. Let me be clear, you'll encounter a lot of strange words, but it's your INTENT that creates magik, and your intent to summon someone like Satan is what counts. If you get all twisted up trying to figure out how these words are said, you'll not accomplish much of anything.

So how do you mitigate these risks? Start with simple rituals and master them. Always double-check your preparations. Think of it like cooking; you wouldn't try to cook a Texas Barbecue Brisket if you've never fried an egg. And never, ever try to barbecue an egg. I'm speaking from experience. Also, protective rituals aren't just for show; they're your spiritual seatbelt.

Now, let's switch gears and talk psychology, but don't yawn. You could be mentally robust, a fortress of a person, but dabbling in high magik can still mess with your mind like nothing else. The energies you engage with can lead to ego inflation, paranoia, or even obsession. Remember, magik is energy, and energy influences matter. Your brain, for all its glory, is matter, and the energies you toy with can essentially rewire your circuits.

I had a friend named Alice. She was amazing, always the life of the party. But she thought she could multitask while performing a complex spell. She believed she could microdose on mushrooms, text her ex, and summon a spirit guide all at the same time. Guess what? She ended up talking to her toaster for a month, thinking it was the reincarnation of Crowley. No joke. She was, what I often call, "tripping balls." Leave the mind-altering herbs to the Shamans, and work magik while sober.

The way to avoid this is to approach magik with the same respect you would give a surgical procedure. Focus is key, people! Before undertaking any magikal work, sit quietly, meditate, and ensure you're psychologically grounded.

The Checks and Balances: Know When to Fold 'Em

Listen, even the most seasoned of us need to know when to step back. There are times when even a small misstep in a ritual can make you feel like you're spiraling down a metaphysical drain. You may be tempted to double down, thinking you can fix it. Sometimes it's better to just halt everything, cleanse your space, and take a break. High magik is a marathon, not a sprint. Remember, it's not about proving you're the biggest sorcerer on the block; it's about a lifelong relationship with energy.

Personally, I now spend way less time in a ritual than I used to. I prefer pathworking, as it's much faster. Once I cover all the topics of magik with His Unholiness, I'll present a few pathworkings to allow you to make contact with The Prince of Darkness minus the trappings of a traditional high magik ceremonial. Don't worry, I'll also show you a few tricks to use to safely work with Satan's energy, avoiding impostors (spirits invading to pretend to be the spirit you summoned) and ejecting unwanted energies out of your space.

So, to recap: the practice of high magik is thrilling but fraught with risks. It's not a playground for the spiritually cocky or the psychologically unprepared. Treat it with the gravitas it deserves, and it will open doors you never knew existed. Skimp on the preparation, focus, or respect, and you could be opening Pandora's Box.

Will you still make mistakes? Of course! Even Merlin had bad beard days. But in the grand tapestry of spiritual evolution, every misstep is a lesson, every error a stepping-stone. So go ahead, step into the world of high magik. Just make sure you've got your boots laced up tight. After all, it's not every day that you dance with the cosmos. And let me tell you, the cosmos has got some seriously fancy footwork.

Fortunately, in my experience, failed magik simply does not work.

It's when it works too well is when it's a problem. (I recounted this story in my Lilith book!)

Chapter 3

Baneful Magik vs. Really Black Magik

There is something truly enchanting and mysterious about the world of magik. Just like an ancient tome that captivates with its charm, and as modern as your latest Instagram filter, this is a truly enchanting experience. Yet, here's where we stumble onto a metaphorical crossroads, my mystical compatriots: the fine line between baneful magik and what we'll daringly label as "Really Black Magik." Kinda sounds like the title of a heavy metal band's debut album.

First, I need to talk about baneful magik. This is the stuff that makes tabloids and midnight horror movies; it's the stuff of curses, hexes, and all those other words that sound like someone sneezed while trying to recite Latin backward. Baneful magik, for all its nefarious connotations, might not always stem from a malicious heart. Sometimes it's more of a "scorched earth" approach to dealing with life's little... ahem... annoyances. Perhaps you've crafted a spell to keep your toxic ex out of your social circle. In such cases, one might argue that the aim isn't so much to harm another, but to protect oneself. A magical version of a restraining order, if you will.

Imagine a friend of mine, let's call her Rebecca. She used to date this guy, 'Steve,' who just couldn't take a hint. Even after they broke up, he would show up uninvited to her hangouts, making everyone uncomfortable. Lisa, a budding practitioner of magik, didn't wish to harm Steve, but she did perform a spell designed to enforce boundaries. A little warding ritual, a hint of protective magik, and voilà—Steve suddenly lost interest in popping up unannounced. Rebecca's intent wasn't malicious; she was merely reclaiming her space. In essence, she used what some may consider "baneful" magik for personal empowerment.

Now let's peek into the darker, shadow-filled corner of Really Black Magik. This kind is wielded with the express intention of causing harm. We're talking spite, we're talking vengeance, and we're talking the kinds of things that even Darth Vader might find a tad extreme. The problem isn't just ethical; it's also practical. Launching a magical assault on someone isn't like sending an angry tweet—you can't just delete it and pretend it didn't happen. Magik, my darlings, has consequences, some of which you can neither foresee nor control. The energies you release into the ether could very well rebound, affecting you in ways you never anticipated.

However, I'm going to stop short of what I call "actual" black magik, the rituals that will make even Satan go "Dude, seriously? That's messed up." Human sacrifice, the type of magik that uses the energy of humans to create the magik. Nope. I'm very much against the use of any living thing being harmed during a ritual.

A while back, another friend, let's call him Mark, decided he'd had enough of his office nemesis, Sarah. She was perpetually one-upping him and generally making his 9-to-5 a living nightmare. So, Mark took it upon himself to whip up a nice, frothy curse. He did it alright, but guess what happened next? His work life didn't improve. In fact, it worsened. The bad vibes he'd sent out ended up isolating him, not just from Sarah, but from other colleagues who used to be friendly with him. He got a cosmic boomerang to the face.

I'm not your grandma, here to wag a finger at you and tell you to play nice. However, it's crucial to understand the monumental difference between using magik as a form of self-empowerment and using it to harm others. One is about enriching your experience and maybe even growing as a person; the other could lead you down a path that's not just dark but perilous.

Let's talk ethics. Say you've got a spellbook, and you find this mind-blowing love spell. You think to yourself, "Wow, imagine the possibilities!" But hold on, hotshot. When it comes to love magik, intent can blur the lines between empowerment and malevolence. Drawing love toward you is one thing, but manipulating someone's will? That's treading on ethically murky grounds, and trust me, the gods and goddesses are watching, probably eating cosmic popcorn but definitely taking notes.

For practitioners of high magik, there's also the Law of Return to consider. It's the magik world's karma, the principle that what you send out energetically will eventually come back to you. If you dish out maliciousness, don't be surprised if you find yourself on the receiving end of some serious cosmic retribution.

The responsibility of wielding magik, especially high magik, cannot be overstated. Remember, magik is neutral. It's a tool, like a pen. You can use it to write love letters or hate mail; the pen doesn't care. But the ink, once spilled, is remarkably hard to clean up. Before you engage in any magik, weigh your intentions carefully. Make sure that you're not just clear on what you want to achieve, but also on the potential repercussions of your actions.

So, there we have it. The world of magik is vast, nuanced, and filled with the potential for both beauty and, well, chaos. Baneful magik and Really Black Magik might seem like two sides of the same cursed coin, but in reality, they are poles apart in their ethical implications and potential impact on your life and the lives of others. Choose wisely, spellcasters. Your next act could either be a triumphant crescendo or a disastrous finale. Either way, the curtain's not coming down anytime soon.

DISTINCTION BETWEEN FREE WILL AND SOUL CONTRACT

You've pondered the ethical implications of baneful magik and what we've colorfully termed "Really Black Magik." Now, as we dig a spade deeper into the esoteric earth, let's discuss another illuminating facet: the line between free will and what's commonly referred to as a soul contract. While both concepts are metaphysical juggernauts in their own right, distinguishing between them can be as tricky as pulling a rabbit out of a hat—without the trick up your sleeve, that is.

Let's start with the notion of free will, the darling principle of every teenage rebellion and indie movie ever. Imagine free will as an unfurled canvas stretched out on a painter's easel, teeming with the intoxicating promise of endless possibilities. Each brushstroke you apply is a conscious choice, a manifestation of your will shape the masterpiece—or sometimes the mess—of your life. For instance, consider the time you decided to practice magik, which was, I dare say, an excellent choice. And yet, the weight of free will extends far beyond mere personal hobbies or weekend plans. In the universe of magik, exercising free will becomes an almost divine act. Here, each incantation is a declaration, each ritual a fortified expression of your autonomy. When you operate under free will, the consequences are yours to bear and the boons yours to enjoy. Yet, as Uncle Ben once wisely advised Spider-Man, "With great power comes great responsibility."

If free will is a canvas, a soul contract is more like an intricate tapestry woven long before you were born—or even before your previous life's cat learned how to climb curtains. A soul contract, gang, is an agreement struck at a soul level, typically before incarnating into this world. These are the big-ticket items of your life: the people you're destined to meet, the challenges you're fated to face, and yes, even the bad hair days preordained by some mischievous cosmic stylist. You can think of soul contracts as the life themes you've signed up to explore, much like choosing a major in college—only you can't switch halfway through the semester because you suddenly find Anthropology dull.

As you might imagine, navigating the complexities of free will and soul contracts in your magik practice can feel like walking a tightrope over a pit of snapping alligators. Have you ever attempted a spell with every fiber of your being yearning for a particular outcome, only to have it result in an inexplicable cosmic fizzle? That's often a clue that what you desire is incongruent with your soul contract. In such cases, it's not your technique that's flawed or your magikal batteries running low; it's simply that you're trying to paint outside the lines of your own cosmic coloring book.

I have several friends and one client who are in lonely life situations. One broke up with a guy and asked me for advice. I did a quick Akashic Record reading and saw that these two had a soul contract to be together. One part was the guy was supposed to deal with his addictive personality and his habit of bailing on relationships after a few years. These two were to get together, and he was to defeat this habit. Instead, he left. I offered to correct the situation using magik. The offer was rejected as it'd violate the guy's free will. It's a delicate situation, and I believe that soul-contracts beat free will, like a full house beats a straight or flush. If I have a client whose soul contract indicates a period of time minus any partner, I'll advise then of this, and suggest it's their free will to counter this, but they'd miss out on any lessons to be learned by being without a partner.

So, what's the takeaway for all you aspiring magicians and cosmic jugglers? It's crucial to learn the art of discernment in your magik practice. Recognize when your actions are an exercise of free will and when they may be bumping up against the sturdier walls of a soul contract. In other words, know when you're free to splatter your canvas with wild abandon, and when it's wiser to follow the pre-sketched lines.

Don't underestimate the importance of this understanding; it's the sort of deep wisdom that separates the novice spellcasters from the sage magik practitioners. The ability to recognize and respect the role of both free will and soul contracts in your magik journey is not just advisable—it's absolutely vital. It shapes not just the outcome of your spells, but the very fabric of your spiritual growth.

And remember, if you ever find yourself frustrated, feeling like you're caught in a magikal quagmire of sorts, consider this: Maybe it's not a question of whether you can do something, but whether you should. After all, magik isn't just about bending the cosmos to your will; sometimes, it's about aligning your will with the cosmos. So go on, take your next magikal step with both caution and courage. Whether you're following the guidelines of your soul contract or painting with the broad strokes of free will, you're still crafting your own extraordinary, otherworldly masterpiece.

LEFT HAND VS. RIGHT HAND PATHS

No book on magik with a spirit like Satan is complete without looking at this subject.

So, what is the distinction between malicious intent and magik serving personal empowerment? The nebulous hinterlands of magik are a place where the distinction between personal empowerment and malicious intent becomes hazy, creating an ethical smog that obscures clear boundaries. Shall we approach this challenging situation with caution and delicacy? Absolutely, let's do it. Prior to delving into the depths of our exploration, dear reader, I implore you to take a moment to fine-tune your energetic shields and realign your moral compass, as the truths we are about to unearth have the potential to profoundly impact your metaphysical foundations.

Fair warning, this might not fully explain everything. This is just one book, you know. This is a real debate, which can, and HAS, caused threads to get deleted and a certain social media site to block a lot of people. I've seen this type of debate blow up, even back when all we had online was a slow modem and telephone lines.

In one corner of this electrifying debate, we have malicious intent. "Bad magik," some call it. You know, the kind where you're tempted to tie someone's fate into knots or maybe banish them to some unpleasant astral zip code. A quick sidebar: Don't. Seriously. Unshackle yourself from this allure before, it becomes a spiritually sticky web from which there's no easy extrication. A binding spell may seem harmless when your intentions feel justified, but remember that the energies you project could boomerang with added umph! You're essentially drawing on the raw, untamed elements of the cosmos and directing them like a focused laser beam. Needless to say, that energy can burn both ways.

Let's talk about Lucy. Lucy, was, or is, a veritable sorceress of the modern age, who also happened to be a friend from my magik circle. Lucy thought she would shortcut her way to workplace success by using magik to oust her rival. "Just a teensy-weensy spell," she reasoned, "What could go wrong?" Famous last words. The fallout was calamitous. Not only did her rival seem even more entrenched, but Lucy's own life spiraled into an abyss of unfortunate events. The universe, guys, keeps a very meticulous ledger. Karma has no statute of limitations, and it always collects—with interest.

Many people might think, Lucy is short for Lucifer. Close. She leveraged magik and it leveraged her back. I can't address the type of ritual it was, but this is a sample of not really thinking things through.

For Lucy, she was unable to distinguish between her own ego and actual pressing issues. She lost quite a few real-life friends, and her followers became cultish. Damn. It was like a cliquish high school drama all over again.

Like I said, this magik is very powerful but needs to be handled with care.

Personal Empowerment: The Selfishness We Need

Then there's the more luminous sister of malicious intent—magik for personal empowerment. It's the self-love spell you cast when you're nursing a broken heart, or the charm you chant for clarity before making a monumental decision. This is not 'selfish' in the way society often mislabels acts of self-care. It's necessary. It's you donning your own oxygen mask before helping others; it's self-preservation in its purest form. It's magik that fuels your soul and refines your energy, transforming you into a conduit of cosmic benevolence.

Here's where the difference becomes crystal—pardon my magikal pun—clear. When you aim for personal empowerment, you elevate your frequency and enrich the collective vibrational tapestry. The energy is additive rather than subtractive. Instead of depleting others, you're contributing to the grand orchestra of spiritual harmonics.

But, and it's a big 'but,' don't mistake personal empowerment for an all-access pass to wield magik indiscriminately. Even seemingly benign intentions can distort when one's inner ethics aren't in equilibrium. Therefore, self-awareness is not a luxury—it's an obligation. Every sigil you sketch, every incantation you whisper, must be aligned with your higher self and congruent with your soul's purpose.

Magikal Ethics: The North Star

Let's bring this home. When we stand at the crossroads of malicious intent and personal empowerment, it's crucial to have a sturdy ethical framework to guide us. What we need is a North Star in this labyrinth of moral ambiguity. Codes like the Wiccan Rede or the Law of Three can serve as that celestial guide, reminding us to be judicious in our magikal pursuits.

So, as we venture forth, navigating the ethereal corridors of magik, let's brandish our wands and athames with not just skill, but wisdom. For in the end, the greatest magik of all is the transformation of ourselves into better, wiser versions of our existence. A spell well cast is one where the metamorphosis occurs within, before manifesting without. And that, cherished reader, is the most profound alchemy of all.

It's a good topic to spark lively debate in some online gathering for magicians… a topic that's sparked countless debates and raised many an eyebrow: the Left-Hand Path and the Right-Hand Path. Okay, debate is too soft a word for the flames that usually result. It's worse than any (NAME) vs (OTHER NAME) argument. Think Nikon vs Canon. Ford vs Chevrolet.

In fact, I forbid this topic in my online magik group.

Anyway, I'm going to try to demystify this seemingly dualistic construct, and illuminate the underlying philosophies that fuel each journey. But a word to the wise: discard your preconceived notions at the door, for you'll need an open mind to traverse this circuitous landscape.

Left-Hand Path: The Rebel's Haven

Magik is often pigeon holed into two main boxes. One is termed the "Left Hand Path" and the other, "Right Hand path." It's not a clear choice, and I'll explain further here in a bit. But first, some simple definitions.

The Left-Hand Path is often shrouded in mystery, controversy, and more than a pinch of societal side-eye. Think of it as the magik of the individualist, the iconoclast, the spiritual rebel. Here, the emphasis is on personal freedom, self-discovery, and the bold assertion of one's own will. You're not so much looking to harmonize with cosmic law as you are attempting to become a law unto yourself. Make no mistake—this isn't the pathway of chaos or destruction, but one of liberation, where boundaries are considered mere suggestions rather than ironclad rules.

Let me share a tale of Marcus, a friend who took the Left-Hand Path, challenging traditional dogmas and rejecting handed-down spiritual mandates. Marcus was always the seeker, the questioner—the one who felt stifled by society's orthodoxies. He cast a series of spells that radically shifted his consciousness, enabling him to shatter the self-imposed chains that society had woven around him. Marcus emerged from his magikal pursuits as someone free from the ordinary constructs of morality and fear, a spiritual being entirely self-authored.

But and this is an important caveat, Marcus was conscientious, always aware of his responsibility toward the energies he wielded. That's the thing about the Left-Hand Path; it's not a free-for-all, but a quest for sovereignty laced with keen self-awareness and ethical nuance.

I personally define the Left Hand as personal empowerment, versus following dogmatic rules, but it's more nuanced than that.

Right-Hand Path: The Path of Unity

In the other corner, we have the Right-Hand Path, which takes a drastically different approach to spirituality and magik. This is the domain of community, altruism, and harmonization with universal energies. Think of it as a cosmic dance, where the aim is to align oneself with the inherent rhythms of the natural world. If the Left-Hand Path is about "me," the Right-Hand Path is certainly about "we."

Here, the operative word is "service." Service to the self, to others, and to the greater cosmic order. It's about polishing your soul until it mirrors the divine, learning to become a more harmonious part of the spiritual symphony that's ceaselessly playing out around us. Those who tread this path often find themselves engaged in magikal acts that benefit not just the self but others, their community, and the Earth itself.

Where Paths Converge: Not All Black and White

Now, these paths are not diametrically opposed, but rather two ends of a complex, often overlapping spectrum. One might even walk both paths at different times or even simultaneously, a spiritual duality that speaks volumes about the intricate, multidimensional nature of human existence. The paths don't shackle you; they offer different sets of tools, different philosophies, and different vistas to explore. Your choice is not set in stone; it's as fluid as your own evolving spirit.

It can be, and often is, combined quite effectively. In fact, this is the basis of my own magik. It's no one else's business except your own.

Your Path, Your Choice

In the end, what matters most is not the path you choose, but how you walk it. Free-will, right? Are you respectful of the energies you wield? Are you considerate of the repercussions that might echo in the unseen corners of reality? And most importantly, are you willing to continually question, to seek, to evolve? Whether Left Hand or Right Hand, the ultimate goal of any magikal journey should be a profound transformation, both within and without. It's not about quick fixes or easy answers; it's about the lifelong process of becoming a more complex, more aware, more empowered spiritual being.

So, choose your path wisely, for this choice will inform your spiritual trajectory, mold your magikal practices, and shape your inner landscape. Whether you're a rebel yearning for untamed spiritual horizons or a healer seeking to mend the frayed fabric of the cosmos, remember that each path offers its own wisdom, its own challenges, and its own unique brand of magik. And that, gang, is the closest thing to a universal truth you'll find in the esoteric world of magik.

THE SATANIC COMPONENT—HOW SATAN FITS WITHIN LEFT-HAND PATH TRADITIONS

Satan, the ever-polarizing figure that has captured the human imagination for centuries, existing as both a boogeyman and a symbol of freedom, depending on whom you ask. Okay ya'll, take a deep breath, because we're about to dissect one of the most misunderstood, yet compelling elements within the Left-Hand Path: the role of Satan, the ultimate archetype of rebellion, freedom, and individualism.

Satan as a Symbol, Not a Deity

To kick things off, let's talk about the fundamental shift in perception that often accompanies one's exploration into Left-Hand Path traditions. Here, Satan is usually not worshipped as a deity in the way mainstream religions worship gods. Rather, he's embraced as a potent symbol of individual empowerment, free will, and resistance against oppressive systems.

For example, the Church of Satan, founded by Anton LaVey in the 1960s, doesn't actually posit the existence of Satan as a supernatural entity. Instead, LaVeyan Satanists see him as a metaphor for human nature—our ambitions, desires, and the innate drive to place ourselves at the center of our own universes. These themes echo loudly within the chambers of the Left-Hand Path, where the self reigns supreme.

A Tale of Transformation

Now, let me share a personal story about Emily, a dear friend who was swept up in the currents of conventional spirituality, following whatever doctrines were offered by the religious gatekeepers of her community. But Emily felt an unshakeable disquiet, an itch she couldn't scratch. And then she encountered Left-Hand Path philosophies and was particularly drawn to the Satanic underpinnings.

In the span of two years, Emily's entire spiritual paradigm shifted. She went from a constant seeker of external validation to someone who found her answers within. Through Satanic symbolism and rituals that focused on self-affirmation and empowerment, she shattered the molds society had cast for her. She stopped seeking a savior and realized she had the power to save herself. It was as if she'd been seeing the world in gray scale, and suddenly it was illuminated in vibrant color. But, and this is crucial, Emily's exploration was coupled with intense study and an intellectual rigor that made her practices deeply grounded. She never took the energies she invoked lightly.

Satan in Historical Context

As we navigate through this subject matter, gaining an understanding of the historical backdrop within which the figure of Satan has developed can offer significant enlightenment. The adversarial archetype we recognize today has roots in Zoroastrianism and the Hebrew Bible, but has been continually co-opted and rebranded, so to speak, throughout history.

In the Gnostic tradition, for instance, Satan or the Demiurge was viewed as an ignorant creator god who trapped human souls in the physical world. These Gnostic undertones can sometimes resurface in Left-Hand Path philosophies that focus on the transcendence of physical limitations and the pursuit of gnosis, or hidden knowledge.

Satan as a Catalyst for Growth

In Left-Hand Path circles, Satan serves as a catalyst for spiritual and psychological growth. Here, interactions with Satanic archetypes or energies are not meant to corrupt, but to challenge. To push one toward a greater understanding of the self, to force an internal confrontation with our own limitations, prejudices, and weaknesses. Satan becomes not the end, but the means to a greater end: the evolution of your own unique spiritual fingerprint.

Potential Misunderstandings and Pitfalls

But caution, dear reader. This path is fraught with potential misunderstandings and pitfalls. The media often portrays Satanic or Left-Hand Path practices as nefarious or evil. However, while there are individuals in any spiritual path who misuse teachings for dark purposes, the Left-Hand Path in general is not about malevolence; it's about growth, self-discovery, and empowerment.

Your Relationship with the Satanic in the Left-Hand Path

The relationship you forge with the Satanic in the context of the Left-Hand Path will be uniquely yours. It's a complex dance with an equally complex partner. Your journey might be rife with confusion, with challenges, perhaps even with moments of fear. But that's just a testament to the transformative power that such a potent symbol, or set of symbols, can wield.

If you choose to engage with Satanic symbolism as part of your spiritual practice, do so with respect, with rigor, and with a keen awareness of both its historical baggage and its liberating potential. The Left-Hand Path beckons not just to any wanderer, but to the brave—those willing to question, to confront, and to transform. Whether Satan becomes a permanent fixture in your spiritual landscape or a transient visitor, the lessons garnered from such an encounter promise to be as transformative as they are unforgettable.

CHAPTER 4

PREPARATIONS FOR RITUAL

Before you start casting a circle and lighting the black candles, a word (or several hundred) on actual preparations for a ritual to the Dark God, Satan.

As I have cautioned in many of my books, don't go into a ritual until your petition is worded correctly, meaning it spells out what you actually want, and the simple conditions of it manifesting, such as "Harming none". Spell out what you wish to manifest as simply as possible, but also making sure any loopholes are covered. Write things like "Please help me manifest twenty thousand American dollars." Spell that out, and indicate the currency. I once worked some magik for some money. In hours, I had found a wallet - no idea who lost it or any ID cards or even slips of paper to help return the wallet to its owner. Inside was a single piece of currency, it was a single bill with $10,000 on it. In Costa Rican currency. It seems I'd forgotten to specify "US Dollars".

It's also good practice to create a sigil from your desire petition, once the petition is simplified into a single sentence. This sigil will serve as a symbolic representation of your intention and will help to focus your energy during the ritual. To create a sigil, start by writing out your desire petition in a clear and concise sentence. Then, remove any duplicate letters and vowels from the sentence, leaving only the consonants.

Next, take the remaining letters and begin to combine and overlap them, creating a unique symbol or design. Allow your intuition to guide you in shaping the sigil, as it should feel personal and meaningful to you. Once you are satisfied with the design, trace it onto a piece of paper or carve it into a small object that you can easily hold during the ritual.

It might look something like this:

The petition is worded differently than the sigil sentence. You'll be asking for your desire in both, but the different wordings are important.

The petition is asking for Satan to bring you the desire. The sigil sentence is worded in the past tense, as if Satan has already delivered.

Thus: Petition is worded "Lord Satan, please help me manifest…."

The sigil is worded: "Lord Satan has given to me ….. "

Note, I say to "manifest". Manifest is just another, more acceptable, word for magik. In the sigil's sentence, I have you put in "Lord Satan", and this ties the desire sigil to his energy.

For a detailed explanation on crafting a sigil, go to my website at Https://Highmagikacademy.com and get my FREE sigil creation course.

However, it does no good to craft a sigil or petition, without first clearly defining your desire.

In any magik, crafting a petition is akin to drawing a map for a treasured journey. It's a preparatory step, a silent conversation between you and the universe, or in cases where you wish to invoke Satan, a dialogue with a force both ancient and enigmatic. This process of defining your desire, particularly when preparing a petition, is a delicate art, balancing between the precision of words and the depth of your true will.

Before you step into the ritual space, before the candles flicker to life and the incantations echo through the night, there's the crucial task of honing your desire into a tangible, clear, and focused petition. This isn't just about what you want; it's about understanding the why, the how, and the potential ripples it might cause in the pond of your existence.

To begin, mindful meditation can serve as a powerful tool. It isn't mandatory, but it's highly beneficial. In the stillness of meditation, allow your mind to quieten and your true desire to rise to the surface. This isn't a rush job; it requires patience and openness. As you meditate, let your thoughts meander around your desire. What does it look like in its purest form? How will it change your life? What are the deeper reasons behind wanting this?

The next step is to articulate this desire into words, and this is where you must tread with care. The language of magik is potent and precise—words are the bones upon which your intentions hang. When drafting your petition, especially in contexts involving Satan, it's imperative to be explicit. Satan, the archetype known for cunning and ambiguity, might just delight in finding the loopholes in your loosely worded desires.

Remember, the specificity of your petition sets the boundaries and defines the path for your desire to manifest. It's like giving clear instructions to a cosmic GPS. If you're too vague, you might end up somewhere you didn't intend to go. So, word your petition with clarity, leaving no room for misinterpretation. It's about crafting a request that aligns perfectly with your will, leaving no space for unintended consequences to sneak in.

Finally, trust plays a pivotal role. Once your petition is crafted, trust in the process, in the magik, and in Satan as the deliverer of your desire, if that's whom you choose to work with. It's a trust that acknowledges the power of the unseen, the unpredictable nature of the universe, and your role as a co-creator in this grand design. Minus this trust, you begin to question the magik. Questioning the magik can stop the magik from working. Period.

In essence, preparing a petition is the foundation of your magikal work. It's the moment where you define the course of your magikal journey, laying down the tracks for where you wish to go. Done with mindfulness, precision, and a deep understanding of your true will, it becomes more than words on paper—it becomes a beacon calling forth the very essence of your desire.

RITUAL ALTAR ITEMS

Now, let's take a brief look at the specific items you'll need for a full High Magik ritual to His Darkness. Most items on the altar are traditional, and they represent the four elements, with the fifth element being your spirit.

Candles represents Fire.

Incense represents Air

Crystals represent Earth

Water in a goblet represents Water.

Including all the elements is a traditional way to set up an altar. Your altar may be against a wall, or in an alcove, and it can be permanent or temporary. The magik will work no matter how the altar is set up. There is no "correct" pattern to set up an altar.

Satan's colors tend towards black, with red. So keep this simple. Black cloth, and red candles.

Altar Cloth

I have several generic cloths I use on my altar. A threadbare green towel (at least 40 years old) is my money altar cloth. I've had this towel since college. I also have a generic triple moon black cloth, with gold printing, and a larger pentacle cloth, black with gold printing.

Candles

On my altar, I'll use two black candles, and two red candles, for Satan or Lilith. If you wish to simplify, use a single black candle. For basic altar candles, one does not need to have a dedicated candle to Satan. If you do, then add a tall red candle to the altar.

Then, you'll need candles for each desire. Consult the appendix for colors associated with specific desires, such as pink for bringing love or granting a wish, red for passion, black for retribution, etc. The ritual specific candle will be lit during the ritual, when the time comes to ask Satan to bless the candle.

Ritual specific candles can be a small chime candle. Or a large glass votive 7-day candle, but this candle is to stay lit until it burns out. So keep that in mind when getting a ritual specific candle.

Burn all candles safely! Make sure the candle isn't near anything flammable, and that it is in a sturdy candle holder. I've had taper candle holders break when the last bits of the candle was burning, so go with metal holders if possible.

The 7-day candles are pretty sturdy, but I have seen one break. I'd put some herbs onto the top of the candle, and it set the entire top on fire and the heat caused the glass to break.

With any glass votive candle, if you want to anoint the candle with an oil, such as money drawing oil, simple place a few drops on the wax on the top. That's all that is needed.

Incense

Incense is a necessary item for every ritual, except pathworking. It acts to sanctify your space and then alters the energy in the space to allow for opening up a small channel for the spirits to enter and communicate with you.

I personally prefer resins burning on a charcoal disc. The type of resin matters as well. Buy a higher quality frankincense. It's an all purpose incense, and is used in place of specific ritual incense. You could also get a sampler pack and see which resins resonate with you. This is your altar, use what you feel works for you.

If you wish to use stick incense, go with any traditional aroma, but avoid overly perfumed or floral incenses. I've used Nag Champa (the spicy one from Om Incense or the blue box with the Guru fella's picture). Nag Champa is an aroma that I used for decades and is always a pleasant choice for a ritual.

Forget essential oils. I was teaching a class on High Magik and several students whined about how they're allergic to incense, so the other person giving the class said it was okay to use essential oil in a diffuser. I said they could try it and report back. It's funny, but the rituals using the oils just didn't work. It's best to totally not use any incense than risk using essential oils and having the spirits not bother to show up. It's as if they're saying "If you can't be bothered to use real incense, I'm not going to bother to show up"

Crystals

The use of crystals on your altar signifies a connection to the Earth element. My choice of tool is limited to just one - a quartz point that I use as my wand. To enhance the energy in your ritual or to symbolize your specific desire, you can choose to place a selection of your favorite crystals on your altar. To find a comprehensive list of crystals and their uses in magik, please refer to the Appendix.

Pen and paper

You will need to write out your petition. There is no special paper or ink required for this purpose. I use a scratch pad from a local pharmacy to write my small petitions and to draw the sigils.

Some texts call for parchment and magik ink. You can, if you wish, obtain some magik paper or ink. Traditionally, parchment is made from the skin of animals, typically sheep, goats, or calves. This process gives it a distinct texture and durability that sets it apart from regular paper. It's not the paper used in baking, plus that paper is hard to write on. In my experiments, it usually didn't work.

Magik ink can also be purchased. I prefer to make my own. I use a blue or red fountain pen ink, then I put a drop or two of my blood into a vial, fill it with the ink, and now it's magik ink.

The pen I usually use is a fountain pen with Ox Blood or Ancient copper ink. This gives the petition and sigil a real medieval occult vibe. However, you can use ANY pen or pencil you choose. It's what you write that is important.

Satan's Sigil

In the back of the book, I have several sigils I've created to Satan, one is a master sigil to be used in every ritual, and will also serve as an offering (when offering a drop of blood). I also have some sigils for specific uses, such as Love, Wealth, Health, and Ascension.

Offerings

This is where most people have difficulty. They get a bit weirded out by the idea of a blood offering. But Satan loves tradition, and a blood offering is the most traditional offering one can give. It's an essence of yourself. Don't worry about the spirit harming you, as the spirit has your DNA. As long as you follow my rituals and summonings, you will get the aspect of Satan you intend to summon.

Like most daemons, Satan loves a blood offering. Not animal blood, but your blood. For a proper offering, while in ritual, you will need a diabetic lancet (sterile and quite sharp) and the Satan master sigil.

Poke a finger (ANY finger...) and drop a single drop or two of your blood onto the sigil. Once this is done, at the correct spot in the ritual, the paper is burned. Use one of the candles and then drop the burning paper into a fireproof bowl. I use a thick ceramic dinner bowl, and I have used two pie tins, one in the other, to burn larger sheets of paper. Keep a spoon or knife handy to stir the ashes to make sure the sigil is completely burned.

Each ritual will also suggest alternate offerings, but at the top of the list will be a blood offering.

Finally, and this is optional, is a small glass or goblet filled with water. With this, the arrangement of all the magik elements are in place and it's time to begin your magik workings.

For this, I'll guide you in the traditional daemonic circle castings and summoning of the elements and their respective daemons. Then I'll present an alternative method of performing the Lesser Banishing of the Pentacle.

Once you have all that down, I'll present a quicker method of accomplishing the same thing, generating a circle of protection and ejecting unwanted or nefarious energy from your space.

TRADITIONAL DAEMONIC CIRCLE CASTING

Method one:

Traditional circles are cast by walking around your altar, first facing north, then to the east, moving clockwise. One invokes the elements, or guardians, of each direction. Traditional Daemonolatry has one draw a specific shape in the air with a finger or athame (knife) or wand.

My standard circle combines all of that and makes it fairly simple. You are still creating a circle of energy designed to keep energy out as well as invite energy in.

For this, I always start the frankincense going. It's very useful to reset the energies in your space. Especially if you use good quality resin or sticks.

Optional: Using a wand or athame. I use my finger, works just as well.

Face North. Deep breath, then walk clockwise around your space, tracing an invisible line with your finger, so that the line encompasses all the space. Once you have walked the circle, face north again.

If your altar is against a wall, or you can't walk around the entire space, VISUALIZE the circle expanding out to totally surround your space, and walk a smaller circle on one side of your altar.

Address the element Earth, represented by the Daemon Belial, face NORTH and say:

Lirach Tasa Vefa Wehlic, Belial

Address the element Air, represented by the Daemon Lucifer, face EAST and say:

Renich Tasa Uberaca Biasa Icar, Lucifer

Address the element Fire, represented by the Daemon Flereous, face SOUTH and say:

Ganic Tasa fubin, Flereous

Address the element Water, represented by the Daemon Leviathan, face WEST and say:

Jedan Tasa hoet naca, Leviathan

Now you have invoked the elements.

In your mind, visualize a bright circle of orange light completely surrounding your space. In your mind, see this light expanding to create a column of light all around you, extending up into the air and into space, and down into the earth, to the planet's core.

You are now ready to start your ritual.

The "standard" Daemonolatry method adds the tracing of the Z-D sigil in the air when facing each direction. Trace the letter "Z" in the air, then circle the "Z" with a "D" by extending the bottom bit of the "Z" up and around to make the "D", then draw your finger down.

You may also trace out a pentagram in the air. It's totally up to you.

Finally, you need to eject unwanted energies

This is the most important step. The last thing you need in your circle is unwanted, negative energies. These energies will interfere with the magick and cause unwanted and unexpected results if it doesn't completely derail the whole thing.

After the circle, I will make a sweeping motion with my out-stretched hands, as if I was gathering up energy and then I'll "toss" the energies out of the space, usually saying:

"All unwanted and invited energies must depart the space now!" You may add any other descriptive phrases that suit you, such as "Begone Jerks!", etc.

SIMPLIFIED METHOD

If you have a private altar space that is not subject to others entering it, then after the first method above, the subsequent rituals may begin with a very simplified cast.

I will face north and visualize the ring of gold energy appearing, surrounding my space, and forming a solid cylinder.

Then I'll simply call on the elements, by turning to face that direction, but without walking around with my finger tracing out the circle.

I still say the ENNs, and call in the Daemons.

PATHWORKING METHOD

This method is to simply sit, and visualize each element arriving, and forming the magick circle. I do this by imagining a small stream forming around me, followed by air swirling over the water, then followed by the water turning to fire, which blazes and forms into bricks.

I then observe a ring of golden light forming, which encircles my space.

LESSER BANISHING (MODIFIED)

Few things in ritual gives a real magik vibe, like performing this LBP, or Lesser Banishing of the Pentacle (or Pentagram). This is my particular version and can be combined with the other circle casting methods.

Stand in the center of your space, facing east.

Relax. Stand with arms at your side.

Close your eyes and raise your right hand above your head, pointing at the ceiling with a finger

Say:

"You are"

With your arm straight, swing your hand in front of you until you are pointing at the floor between your feet

Say:

"This Universe."

Still pointing at the floor, bend your elbow and bring your hand up until you are pointing at your right shoulder

Say;

"The Power"

Move your hand across your chest and point at your left shoulder

Say:

"And The Glory"

Bring both palms together to your chest (as if in prayer)

Say:

"Forever, So be it"

Return your left hand to the side and point directly in front of you with your right hand (like pointing at the rising sun or moon)

Make a small circle in front of you, clockwise, and say:

"Tetra"

Now, move to face the south, and repeat the circle and say:

"Gram"

Again, move to face the west and make the small circle, saying;

"Mut"

Turn to the north, and repeat the circle motion, saying:

"Ton"

Turn so that you are facing east again.

Using the finger of your right hand, make a huge pentagram (or star) in the air in front of you

Now say:

"I send from this place all intruding forces. They shall go far away and be powerless to interfere with my wishes, my thoughts, or my emotion. So be It!"

CHAPTER 5

LOVE AND ROMANCE MAGIK WITH SATAN

If the notion of associating Satan with love spells and romance rituals surprises you, you're not alone. It's a topic that frequently raises eyebrows and churns the pot of public opinion. But strap in, because what follows may reshape your understanding of love, desire, and the Satanic archetype in a magikal context.

First, let's tackle the immediate association people make when Satan comes to mind: evil, malice, and so on. Yet within the complex tapestry of Left-Hand Path practices, Satan represents the pure, unbridled passion that exists in each of us. And what is love, if not one of the most potent forms of human passion? Just as the many gods and goddesses in various traditions oversee various aspects of life, love, and fertility, Satan, too, can preside over rituals designed to attract love or enhance romance.

One might argue that the Satanic is fundamentally rooted in the principle of individual empowerment. It's about recognizing your desires and taking actions—magikal or otherwise—to fulfill them. It's not so much about manipulating someone else's will as it is about changing your own reality to attract what you seek.

Now, let's think about love spells for a moment. The desire to be loved is universal. It transcends culture, age, gender, and even species. But to desire love from a specific person becomes a more complex issue. Is it ethical? Is it effective? What role does consent play?

Within the Left-Hand Path, the focus is typically on personal transformation rather than controlling another. So, a love spell within this framework would probably focus more on making you more lovable or helping you open up to love, rather than forcing someone to fall in love with you.

A Story of Satanic Love Magik

Let me share the story of Mark, someone I know who ventured down this path. Mark had a history of failed relationships. He was desperate for love, but couldn't grasp why he remained single. Discovering the Left-Hand Path philosophies opened a new door for him. The practices he adopted weren't aimed at making a particular person fall in love with him. Rather, they were about unlocking the aspects of himself that were blocking love from entering his life.

With Satan as a symbol of unrestrained desire and passion, Mark crafted a ritual that was as much psychological as it was magikal. It involved a mirror, symbolizing self-reflection; a red candle for passion; and a piece of paper on which he wrote down the traits he felt were blocking his path to love. He recited an invocation to Satan—not as a deity to be worshipped, but as an embodiment of the passion he wished to unleash. He then safely burned the paper in the flame of the red candle, symbolizing the eradication of these barriers.

Months later, Mark found himself in a fulfilling relationship. He attributes this not to the manipulation of his partner's will but to the change in himself, a change catalyzed by his Satanic ritual.

When approaching Satanic magik for love and romance, one has to be aware of ethical implications. Just because you can, doesn't mean you should. In Left-Hand Path traditions, personal responsibility is paramount. While you're working to attract love, remember that love is a two-way street that involves consent and mutual attraction.

ETHICAL CONSIDERATIONS IN LOVE MAGIK

So, you're intrigued by the potential of love magik. The candles are glowing, incense wafts through the air, and your chosen words of power resonate with the energy you're trying to harness. But wait—before you reach for that vial of rose oil, let's pause. In the charged, pulse-quickening domain of love magik, ethics is a subject we cannot ignore. The purpose of this chapter isn't to throw a wet blanket on your fire of enthusiasm; instead, think of it as a guidepost that adds layers of responsibility and wisdom to your practices. In this chapter, let's talk about love magik, with all its pitfalls and pleasures, through the lens of ethics.

Firstly, what does "ethics" even mean in a magikal context? It's not a one-size-fits-all concept. But at its core, ethics concerns itself with what one should do, not just what one can do. And in the vast world of magik, this could mean everything from respecting someone's free will to responsibly sourcing your ritual materials.

Let's start with a big one: consent. Picture yourself whispering sweet incantations under the moonlight to make someone—let's call them Taylor—fall in love with you. Sounds romantic, right? But let's flip the coin for a moment. What if Taylor were the one casting the spell, aiming to bend your emotions to their will? Not so enchanting now, is it?

Consent is key. And while the idea of orchestrating an unsolicited love connection might sound tempting, the ethical implications can be complicated, to say the least. Magik that aims to influence another person's feelings can be intrusive. Respect for individual autonomy and free will should remain front and center in any love magik operation.

Do No Harm, Take No Harm

The credo "Do no harm" resonates across many spiritual and magikal practices, and for a good reason. It serves as a reminder to consider the broader impact of our actions. If a love spell inadvertently causes a rift between Taylor and their current partner, leading to emotional turmoil for both, then your magik has likely caused more harm than good. Always remember, love magik should uplift, not disrupt.

Free-Will and Soul Contracts in Love Magik

I've previously written about this: Free-will versus soul contracts. And this is where lively discussion usually ensues, especially online.

While at first glance they may seem at odds with each other, they weave together in complex ways, especially when it comes to matters of the heart. Understanding the intricate interplay between these two elements is crucial for anyone engaging in love magik, both for ethical implications and the effectiveness of the magikal work itself.

Firstly, let's discuss free-will. One of the most ethically charged debates in love magik centers around the concept of free-will—the ability of individuals to make choices unencumbered by external influence. Practitioners of love magik must be exceptionally careful not to infringe upon another person's free-will. For instance, casting a spell to make someone fall in love with you without their consent is considered not just ethically dubious, but also fundamentally invasive. It risks causing harm by manipulating emotions and creating bonds that aren't naturally forged.

Now, let's move onto the intriguing notion of soul contracts. These are agreements made on a spiritual plane that influence our lives in the earthly dimension. Some believe that certain relationships are predestined, arranged before birth to facilitate growth, learning, or karmic resolution. When conducting love magik, it's essential to ponder whether the love you're seeking aligns with these spiritual contracts. Some spells and rituals might be ineffective, not because they're executed poorly, but because they contradict a soul contract, causing unnecessary complications.

So, how do free-will and soul contracts intertwine? If we are bound by pre-existing soul contracts, is free-will just an illusion? Not necessarily. Consider soul contracts as frameworks, setting up specific conditions and relationships that guide our life journey. However, within those parameters, we exercise free-will in how we navigate those relationships and what decisions we make. In the context of love magik, this means that while a spell might align with a soul contract and facilitate a relationship, the way that relationship manifests and evolves is still subject to the free-will of the individuals involved.

Understanding the dance between free-will and soul contracts enriches the ethical and spiritual dimensions of love magik. It adds layers of complexity that demand thoughtful contemplation, ensuring that the magik you perform is not only effective but also respectful of both earthly autonomy and cosmic design.

Then add in the idea that one can attempt to enforce a soul contract with another using magik, yet this might seem to violate free-will. It does! But, when you consider that soul contracts often trump free-will, especially in magik, this is almost a "get out of jail" card.

Self-Love: An Ethical Alternative

Interestingly, love magik doesn't have to involve another person. Many people find great success—and encounter far fewer ethical dilemmas—when they target their love magik towards themselves. Enhancing your own qualities to make you more receptive to love not only sidesteps the issue of consent but also puts you in a position to attract love more naturally.

The downside to this is accidental allowing an opening for scam artists to enter your life, and take advantage of you. Especially if you're older. It's why I rarely "friend" or "follow" anyone who's suspiciously too young for me, and appear too eager to "be my friend." Use caution. Check the other person out carefully, especially in this modern world of social media.

When performing any ritual, you're putting energy out into the world. And that energy will, in some form, return to you. Some call this the Law of Return, the Principle of Cause and Effect, or simply karma. Even if you don't subscribe to these concepts, consider the psychological impact. Knowing that you manipulated someone can plant a seed of doubt and insecurity that gnaws at the relationship. Ask yourself: is it worth it?

It's not just about the ethics concerning the people involved; it's also about where your magikal supplies come from. Your rose petals, crystals, or that beautiful wooden wand—they all originated from the earth or from artisans who crafted them. Consider their origins and strive for sustainability and fair trade. Ethics should extend beyond the ritual space into all areas of practice.

While there are some generally agreed-upon "do's and don't's", ethics in magik can be a very personal thing. Your individual moral compass should guide you, and your practices should evolve as you gain experience and insight. Some may advocate for "white magik" as a purely beneficial force, while others will tell you that magik has no color—it simply is. Wherever you stand, the idea is to act responsibly and consider the potential outcomes of your magikal work.

Fine-Tuning Your Ethical Compass

As you continue down your magikal path, your understanding of ethics will likely deepen and become more nuanced. You'll learn from both successes and mistakes, and that's okay. What's important is that you're asking these questions, engaging in self-reflection and always striving to act in a way that's aligned with your evolving understanding of what's right and responsible.

In the end, love magik should be a force for good in your life. It should bring joy, not just to you, but to others around you. It's a powerful tool, and like any tool, it can be used both constructively and destructively. That's why I've dedicated an entire chapter to the subject of ethics. If love is the essence that fuels your magik, let ethics be the compass that guides its course.

Each chapter brings you closer to understanding the richness and the responsibilities of a life adorned with magik. As you continue to read, remember that ethical considerations are not just guidelines but reflections of your deeper values. They enrich your practice and elevate it from mere technique to a path of wisdom. Let's journey together into the following chapters with eyes wide open, and hearts ready for the ethical enchantment that awaits.

SIMPLE LOVE SPELLS

So, spells or rituals?

The practice of love magik often raises the question: what is the difference between spells and rituals? While these terms are sometimes used interchangeably, they are, in fact, distinct in their purposes, execution, and energy dynamics.

Understanding these differences can be pivotal in deciding the most effective route for your magikal endeavor, especially when matters of the heart are involved.

Love Spells

Love spells are specific sets of actions designed to channel energy toward a clearly defined goal—be it attracting a new partner, rejuvenating an existing relationship, or even fostering self-love. A spell generally uses items like candles, herbs, and crystals to help focus this energy. Often considered to be the "quicker" form of magik, spells are usually simple to perform and tend to focus on immediate, tangible results. They can be as uncomplicated as saying a chant while holding a rose quartz or as elaborate as a multi-day candle magik spell. The effectiveness of a love spell relies heavily on the practitioner's intent, their concentration, and the specificity of their goal. Since spells are focused on bringing about change in the physical world, it's crucial to remember the ethical considerations we discussed earlier regarding free-will and soul contracts.

Love Rituals

Rituals, on the other hand, are more complex and often serve broader, less tangible goals. Unlike spells, which are typically geared toward creating a specific outcome, rituals are generally designed to align oneself with a particular energy or universal principle. They involve a series of actions or procedures that one must follow in a particular order, often including prayer, meditation, and offerings. Love rituals might aim to enhance one's overall love life, improve emotional well-being, or open oneself to the possibility of future love, rather than trying to affect a single, concrete outcome.

Rituals often tap into archetypes and deities, invoking their presence or assistance in the magikal working. This could involve calling upon Aphrodite for enhancing romantic energy or invoking Hades and Persephone for a relationship that has a transformative potential. The inherent complexity and structure of a ritual provide space for deep spiritual connection, and thus, they are often preferred for more enduring and less immediate objectives.

Key Distinctions

So, in summary, spells are more outcome-oriented, quick, and focused on the material plane. Rituals are more process-oriented, complex, and aimed at broader, more spiritual goals. While a love spell might be employed to find a date for Saturday night, a love ritual might be more appropriate for someone looking to heal from past relationship trauma or to understand their romantic needs better.

Both spells and rituals with Satan bring their own ethical quandaries. The figure of Satan has long been associated with challenging conventional moral standards, which can be both liberating and risky. For instance, the practitioner must ponder whether invoking a figure as polarizing as Satan might, in itself, impact the free will of others involved. This becomes doubly important in the context of love magik, which already teeters on the edges of free will and manipulation.

Love spells with Satan tend to be more tactical, aimed at achieving specific romantic results quickly. In contrast, love rituals with Satan are broader in scope and work on deeper, more spiritual aspects of your love life. While both are powerful methods of employing magik, they serve different objectives and thus require different levels of commitment, preparation, and ethical consideration.

The key to successful love magik with Satan lies in balancing your desires with respect for the will of others and understanding the potent energies you are working with. Make sure to approach either route with caution, reverence, and a deep sense of responsibility.

5 SIMPLE LOVE SPELLS USING SATAN

Engaging with Satan in love magik is not something to be taken lightly, but it can be extremely potent. Each of these spells is designed for specific purposes. As with any magikal practice involving powerful figures, make sure your intentions are clear and you are ready to handle the energies you invoke.

Spell 1: Attract a New Love

Items Needed:

    A red candle

    Rose petals

    Parchment paper

    Red ink pen

    A small piece of rose quartz

Actions:

Light the red candle and place the rose quartz next to it.

Write your intent or wish for a new love on the parchment paper using red ink.

Scatter the rose petals around the candle.

Speak your intent aloud, invoking Satan to aid you in your quest for love.

Let the candle burn out naturally.

Spell 2: Boost Romantic Confidence

Items Needed:
    A mirror
    Lavender oil
    A black candle
    A small bowl

Actions:
    Light the black candle and place it before the mirror.

    Dab lavender oil on your wrists and neck.

    Look at yourself in the mirror and affirm your self-love and attractiveness.

    Invoke Satan to amplify your inner power and boost your romantic confidence.

    Snuff out the candle after you feel a surge of self-assurance.

Spell 3: Rekindle Passion in a Relationship

Items Needed:

Two small red candles

Cinnamon sticks

Photos of you and your partner

Actions:

Light the two red candles and place them on either side of the photos.

Lay cinnamon sticks across the photos.

Call upon Satan to reignite the passion in your relationship.

Allow the candles to burn down while focusing on the love you share with your partner.

Spell 4: Cut Ties with an Ex-Lover

Items Needed:

A black string

A small piece of paper

A fireproof bowl

A white candle

Actions:

Write the name of your ex-lover on the piece of paper.

Tie the paper with black string.

Light the white candle.

Invoke Satan to sever emotional ties with the named individual.

Burn the paper in the fireproof bowl, letting go of past energies.

Spell 5: Attract Genuine Connection

Items Needed:

A yellow candle

A magnet

Jasmine incense

Actions:

Light the jasmine incense and the yellow candle.

Place the magnet next to the candle.

As the incense fills the room, focus on your desire for a genuine, meaningful relationship.

Call upon Satan to attract connections that resonate with your soul.

Let the candle burn out completely.

Remember, the core of any spell is your intention. Make sure your intentions align with the energies you are calling upon, especially when dealing with a figure as potent and transformative as Satan. Always be conscious of the ethical implications of your actions.

LOVE RITUALS

If love spells are the sprinters, then rituals are the marathon runners. These are intricate ceremonies with eyes on the long game or higher spiritual aims. Bringing Satan into a love ritual aims for transformation at a foundational level, targeting deeper self-understanding, self-appreciation, or a complete overhaul of your love life. You're not just asking for a quick favor from Satan; you're requesting guidance through a life-altering journey. This might mean confronting your own relational hang-ups or escaping societal constructs that have limited your love life. The groundwork for rituals is usually elaborate, involving consecrated spaces, prolonged meditations, and multiple summonings.

Now, it's not all hearts and roses. Involving Satan in love spells and rituals comes with its own ethical baggage. Known for questioning traditional morals, Satan's influence can be both freeing and perilous. As a practitioner, you must seriously contemplate whether invoking such a divisive figure might inadvertently override someone else's free will. This is especially crucial when it comes to love magik, which dances a fine line between free will and coercion.

Love spells that involve Satan are like tactical strikes— quick, precise, and outcome-focused. In contrast, love rituals with Satan are grander in scope, emphasizing the spiritual and foundational elements of love. Each approach is potent in its own right but serves different purposes, necessitating varying degrees of focus, preparation, and ethical scrutiny.

Ultimately, the success of your love magik with Satan hinges on aligning your personal desires with a deep respect for others' free will, while being fully aware of the robust energies at play. Whatever your method, proceed with mindfulness, reverence, and a profound sense of responsibility.

With love magik, Satan often plays a role that is both enigmatic and deeply misunderstood. Engaging with such a potent figure in love rituals requires not only a deep understanding of the magikal arts but also a nuanced grasp of the nature of love itself. This exploration takes us on a profound journey into the complexities of participating in love rituals with Satan, an endeavor that intricately merges the elements of desire, transformation, and the profound depths of the human heart.

Love rituals are elaborate ceremonies that extend beyond the immediacy of spells. They are not mere tools for attracting a partner or igniting a spark of passion; they are transformative experiences that seek to align your deepest desires with the cosmic energies. Involving Satan in these rituals means tapping into a powerful archetype known for breaking boundaries and challenging conventional notions of love and relationships.

Let's begin.

As with ANY magik, the preparation for a love ritual with Satan is as crucial as the ritual itself. It begins with setting the right atmosphere, one that resonates with the energies you wish to invoke. This may include creating a sacred space adorned with symbols and items that represent love, passion, and transformation. Red and black candles, a chalice of wine, and an array of crystals like rose quartz or garnet can be used to set the stage.

Now, you need to focus on crafting your intent. The heart of any ritual lies in the intent behind it. With Satan, this intent needs to be articulated with precision and clarity. Are you seeking to break free from past romantic traumas? Do you wish to uncover the deepest desires of your heart, or are you looking for a transformation in how you experience love? The clearer your intent, the more focused the energy of the ritual.

Let's take a look at two examples of love rituals with the Prince of Darkness. In a later chapter on influencing people, we'll look at some love/sex rituals where you can compel someone to your side. In the meantime, here's some interesting rituals for love.

Feel free to modify these rituals. However, do not modify the actual summoning, as you're calling upon an aspect of Satan which handles this magik.

RITUAL 1: ATTRACTING TRUE LOVE

This ritual is designed to invoke the energies associated with Satan to draw a lover into your life. It emphasizes the importance of clear intent and ethical practice. Remember, the goal is to attract love that is mutually beneficial and respectful of free will. For this, you'll need to access running water, like a stream, to close the ritual. This sends the petition into the earth (Gaia's) magik system.

What sets this apart from my usual ritual is you craft your petition while in ritual.

For this, we'll use a different offering. As suggested by his Unholiness, a small amount of red wine, a small amount of an excellent whiskey, or an offering of sweet bread, such as a piece of cake or an iced breakfast roll.

Items Needed:

Black and red candles (two of each is recommended)

A mirror

A piece of parchment or writing paper

A red ink pen (permanent, not fountain pen ink)

Rose petals

Satan's master Sigil

Offering (we're skipping the blood offering)

Arrange the black and red candles in a semi-circle around the mirror. Light them to begin your ritual. Turn off the room lights. Light the incense.

Sit in front of the mirror and gaze into your reflection, allowing your thoughts to focus on your deepest desires in love.

Take the piece of parchment and, using the red ink pen, write down the qualities you seek in a partner or the aspects of love you wish to attract or enhance in your life. Keep it simple, but make sure to go into some details. Things like "emotionally available" is a good condition. I'd even recommend stating explicitly which gender your desired partner is. You know, just to be safe.

Invoke Satan's God aspect in this ritual by using his summoning:

Lord Satan! Ave Satanis!

Ave Tasa Bunis La Satan!

Ave Tasa Bunis La Satan!

Ave Tasa Bunis La Satan!

I ask you to be with me and hear my prayer!

At this time, scatter rose petals around the base of the mirror, symbolizing the blossoming of love and desire.

Read your written desires aloud, then fold the parchment and place it in the bowl of water. This act symbolizes the fluidity and evolving nature of love. It'll also cause the ink to run, so use a ball-point pen or permanent marker.

Now, give the offering to Satan by placing the wine or food on his master sigil.

When giving the offering, say:

Lord Satan, please accept this humble offering in gratitude for your attention to this request!

Allow this to stay overnight, then dispose of the offering outside.

Extinguish the candles one by one, symbolically sealing your ritual and sending your desires into the universe.

Store the parchment in a safe place until your desires begin to manifest, then locate a spot with a stream or running water, and release the parchment into the water, thanking Satan for his guidance.

RITUAL 2: BREAKING PAST RELATIONSHIP BONDS

Getting rid of the energy of past relationships, breaking those bonds, is a first step in attracting a new love into your life. For this, you'll need your ex's photo, or a symbol of them. Craft your petition statement like this: *"Lord Satan! I now ask that you assist me in moving on from my relationship with _____. I ask that this be done safely, with harm to none!"*

Write this on any paper, using a red pen. You might also craft a sigil from this statement, wording it in the past tense.

We'll be using the traditional summoning of Satan, who is quite good at this type of magik.

Items Needed:

A black candle

A representation of your past relationship (e.g., a photo or symbolic item)

Salt

An obsidian stone

A fireproof container

Offering & Fireproof bowl/ diabetic lancet

Sigil for desire

Satan's Egregore Sigil

When ready, light the altar candles and switch off the room's lights.

Start the incense.

Summon Satan:

Tasa reme laris Satan – Ave Satanis

Tasa reme laris Satan – Ave Satanis

Tasa reme laris Satan – Ave Satanis

Lord Satan! I summon thee!

Be with me in my space, at this time!

Now, light the black candle, signifying protection and the banishment of negative energies.

Place the representation of your past relationship in front of the candle.

Circle the representation with salt, creating a boundary and symbolically purifying your life from past influences.

Hold the obsidian stone, known for its properties of releasing negativity and emotional blockages. Meditate on releasing the bonds of your past relationship.

Carefully, and with intent, burn the representation in the fireproof container. As it burns, invoke Satan to aid in cutting these emotional ties and to empower you with strength and clarity, moving forward.

Present your offering to Satan. Prick a finger and place a single drop of blood onto the master sigil.

Say: ***"Please accept this humble offering of my essence, in gratitude for working to manifest my desire!"***

Touch the edge of the sigil to a candle and allow the sigil to be fully burned.

Extinguish the candle, visualizing the final severance of past emotional bonds.

Keep the obsidian stone with you in the coming days as a reminder of your ritual and the strength you possess.

Remember, this ritual is about aligning your energies with the potential for love in your life, inviting it in a respectful, harmonious way. Approach it with sincerity, hope, and an open heart.

All of these rituals require introspection and honesty, and while invoking Satan, it is crucial to approach with a clear mind and heart, ensuring your intentions align with your highest good and respecting the natural law of free will.

The aftermath of a love ritual with Satan is often a time of reflection and integration. You may find that your perspectives on love and relationships have shifted. There might be a newfound clarity or a sense of empowerment in how you approach matters of the heart.

Ethical Considerations

It's vital to approach these rituals with an ethical mindset. Remember, the goal is not to manipulate or coerce, but to grow, understand, and transform. The energies you work with, especially when involving a figure like Satan, are potent and demand respect and responsibility.

Final Thoughts

Engaging in love rituals with Satan is a journey into the depths of your own heart, mirrored against the backdrop of a powerful, transformative archetype. It's a path that demands courage, honesty, and a willingness to face the unknown. When approached with respect, clarity, and ethical consideration, such rituals can be a profound tool for personal transformation and a deeper understanding of love's true nature.

CHAPTER 6

MONEY AND PROSPERITY MAGIK WITH SATAN

In the labyrinthine world of magik, the pursuit of material wealth can be a complex and intriguing path, especially when it intersects with entities like Satan. Often cloaked in misconception, invoking Satan for financial prosperity requires a nuanced understanding of both the figure and the nature of material gain itself.

The Intricacies of Invoking Satan for Wealth

Imagine standing at a crossroads, one path shimmering with the promise of material riches, the other winding into the mysteries of the spiritual realm. At this juncture, you find Satan, a figure often associated with temptation and earthly desires. But there's more to this iconic entity than meets the eye. In many Left-Hand Path traditions, Satan is not just a symbol of indulgence but also of empowerment and breaking free from self-imposed limitations. He embodies the untamed, ambitious spirit that dares to desire more.

Crafting Your Approach

When you decide to invoke Satan for financial prosperity, it's essential to approach with clarity and respect. You're not simply asking for a cash windfall; you're seeking to unlock the potential for wealth that resides within you and around you. It's a request to open doors, to illuminate opportunities, and to embolden your own ability to seize them.

It does no good, in the long haul, to invoke Satan for some quick cash, only to have to invoke him again the next month! Look ahead, plan. Don't wait until your world is falling apart to invoke Satan for a quick fix. Yes, he does work quickly, but it's best to set some long-range goals, and work towards those.

The Dance of Material and Spiritual

At its core, working with Satan for material gain is a dance between the spiritual and the material realms. It's acknowledging that while wealth and possessions are of the physical world, the power to attract and manifest them originates from a deeper spiritual source. The key is to maintain a balance, to use material gains not as an end in themselves but as tools for furthering your own growth and, ideally, contributing positively to the world around you.

Satan as a Catalyst for Change

In this journey, Satan becomes a catalyst, sparking the transformation from a state of lack or contentment to one of abundance and prosperity. This transformation is not merely about padding your bank account; it's about redefining your relationship with money, wealth, and success. It's about shifting from a mindset of scarcity to one of abundance.

The Rituals Ahead

Throughout the course of this chapter, our focus will shift towards a more detailed examination of various rituals that have been proven to enhance income levels and draw in substantial amounts of money. These rituals are not just about chanting incantations or lighting candles; they are about aligning your energies with the frequencies of abundance and prosperity. They are about casting off old beliefs that have shackled your financial potential and embracing a new paradigm where wealth flows freely towards you.

Embarking on this path with Satan requires courage and an open mind. It's about stepping beyond the boundaries of conventional morality and daring to claim the prosperity that the universe has in store for you. As you turn the pages and uncover the rituals that lie ahead, remember that you are not just performing magik; you are initiating a profound transformation in your life, one where wealth and spirituality coalesce into a harmonious symphony. Let's begin this journey together, with an open heart and an unwavering resolve to unlock the doors of prosperity and abundance.

But first, let's examine the concept of money and how magik works in this regard.

When navigating the intricate world of magik, particularly in relation to figures such as Satan, it becomes apparent that the boundary separating the material and spiritual realms is as fragile as a spider's silk, yet its significance rivals the immense chasm that exists between heaven and earth. Understanding and maintaining this balance is crucial, not just for the success of your magikal workings, but for your overall spiritual health. Let's look at this delicate equilibrium between the pursuit of material wealth and the nourishment of the soul.

THE DUAL NATURE OF WEALTH

Life, like a grand theater, is a place where the boundaries of reality and magic often merge, and within this captivating realm, wealth takes the form of a coin, showcasing its two distinct yet inseparable sides. Reflecting the duality of our existence, this coin, which serves as a metaphorical embodiment of wealth in its entirety, gracefully spins through the vast expanse of the cosmos. Together, let's take a closer look at this allegory and explore the intricate layers that unveil the true essence of what genuine wealth signifies.

On one gleaming side of this mystical coin, we find the tangible. Here lies the kingdom of material possessions - money, property, and all those glittering artifacts that humankind has long since equated with success and comfort. This side of the coin is the domain of the palpable, the stuff that you can touch, feel, and flaunt. It's the security of a bank balance that promises a life free from want, the solidity of four walls that shelter dreams and aspirations, and the comfort of worldly possessions that whisper promises of happiness and ease. In the physical space, this side of the coin reigns supreme, glistening with the allure of certainty and the promise of power.

Flip the coin, and you're faced with an entirely different aspect of wealth - the spiritual. This side is less about what you can hold in your hands and more about what you hold in your heart. It's the wealth of fulfillment, happiness, and inner peace. Unlike its material counterpart, this side doesn't jingle in your pocket or glitter in bank vaults. Instead, it resonates in the harmonious melodies of your soul. Here lies the joy that comes from knowing you are living your life in alignment with your true purpose, the tranquility that blooms from understanding your place in the universe, and the fulfillment that arises from connecting deeply with others and with your own inner self. This spiritual wealth is about enrichment of a different kind - not of your wallet, but of your being.

True wealth, in its most holistic sense, is the perfect balance of these two sides. It's the understanding that material prosperity can provide comfort and opportunities to grow, but without spiritual richness, such comfort can be as hollow as a drum. Conversely, spiritual wealth without the grounding of material stability can leave one unmoored, floating adrift in a sea of ideals without the means to manifest them.

In the dance of life, we are constantly flipping this coin, shifting our focus between material gains and spiritual growth. The art, then, is not to favor one side of the coin over the other, but to let them both spin in harmony, creating a dynamic equilibrium where each aspect enhances the other. It's recognizing that material wealth can be used as a tool to foster spiritual growth and that spiritual wealth can bring a sense of fulfillment that no amount of money can buy.

As we journey through the chapters of our lives, let's keep this coin spinning, always striving for that delicate balance where material wealth meets spiritual abundance, and together, they create the symphony of a life well-lived.

Materiality in Magik

Many individuals venture down the path of seeking material gains in the mystical world of the occult and magik, particularly when they invoke powerful entities such as Satan. This journey, woven deeply into the fabric of many magikal practices, revolves significantly around the physical manifestation of wealth. It's a world where the incantation of spells, the lighting of candles, and the casting of sigils become the tools to draw forth prosperity, unlock doors to new financial opportunities, and manifest abundance in its most tangible forms.

Let's look deeper into this aspect of materiality in magik. When one invokes Satan for material gain, they tap into an ancient, primal force that embodies the power to effect a change in the physical world. This involves calling upon energies that resonate with the material desires of the practitioner. The aim could be as specific as seeking a new job, a financial windfall, or even the acquisition of property and assets. The rituals and spells used in this context are meticulously crafted to align one's personal energy with the frequencies of wealth and abundance.

However, this pursuit of material wealth in the world of magik is not without its pitfalls. It becomes a double-edged sword when the focus solely lies on accumulating material wealth, overshadowing the crucial balance with one's spiritual well-being. In such instances, the practitioner might find themselves akin to a gardener who tends to only one corner of their garden. They may water this section, nurture it, and watch it flourish, but in doing so, they neglect the rest of their garden. The result is an unbalanced landscape where one part thrives while the rest withers.

This metaphor extends seamlessly into the practice of magik. Focusing only on material gains can lead to a spiritual drought. The neglected parts of the garden represent the facets of one's life that also require nourishment – personal growth, emotional health, and spiritual development. Without attending to these, the practitioner might find themselves in a lush but ultimately unfulfilling paradise. They may achieve financial success, but without spiritual balance, it can feel hollow, leaving them disconnected from the deeper, more meaningful aspects of life.

In magik, as in nature, balance is key. The flourishing of a garden, or in this case, one's life, depends on the harmonious nurturing of both the material and the spiritual. Engaging in practices that not only draw material wealth but also foster spiritual growth and personal development ensures that all aspects of life are given the opportunity to thrive. Just as a well-tended garden blooms in all its sections, a well-balanced magikal practice enriches both the physical and the spiritual domains of the practitioner.

As we continue to explore the complex interplay between materiality and spirituality in magik, it becomes clear that the true mastery of the art lies in finding equilibrium between these two worlds. It's about understanding that material prosperity is a means, not an end, and that true fulfillment often lies in the unity of material success and spiritual enlightenment.

Spirituality: The Undercurrent

In the intricate dance of magik, particularly when it intertwines with the pursuit of wealth, spirituality emerges not as an adversary to material abundance, but as its essential counterpart. This notion of spirituality is far from the idea of renouncing worldly possessions. Instead, it invites a deeper understanding of the role that material wealth plays in the grand tapestry of existence. It's an acknowledgment that while the accumulation of wealth can undeniably make the journey of life more comfortable, it is the essence of spiritual richness that infuses this comfort with true meaning and fulfillment.

Picture material wealth as a luxurious vessel sailing across the vast ocean of life. It is grand and impressive, equipped with all the amenities for a comfortable journey. However, without the anchor of spirituality, this magnificent ship is at the mercy of the ocean's capricious nature, floating aimlessly, vulnerable to the tempestuous whims of the sea. Spirituality, in this metaphor, is the anchor that provides stability and direction. It ensures that, while the journey is comfortable; it is also purposeful and grounded.

When integrating Satan into your magikal practice for wealth, it becomes essential to recognize and respect this duality. The archetype of Satan, often misconstrued, encompasses far more than the mere pursuit of material desires. Satan represents the human struggle for meaning, identity, and understanding in a reality that is often overwhelmingly materialistic. This entity symbolizes the challenge of navigating a world where material temptations are incessant and alluring.

Invoking Satan in the quest for wealth, therefore, transcends the mere act of seeking financial prosperity. It becomes a complex ritual where the request for abundance is intertwined with a yearning for wisdom and spiritual balance. It's an appeal for the discernment to utilize the wealth in ways that are not just personally beneficial but also spiritually enriching. The practitioner seeks not only the fulfillment of material desires but also the insight to maintain a harmonious balance between their worldly pursuits and their spiritual well-being.

In essence, when you call upon Satan to aid in your financial endeavors, you are doing more than asking for an increase in your bank balance; you are seeking guidance in navigating the often turbulent waters of material gain. You are asking for the wisdom to use your wealth in ways that contribute to your growth and fulfillment, not just as a magikal practitioner, but as a human being seeking a deeper connection with the universe. This approach ensures that the pursuit of wealth is not a hollow endeavor but a journey that is as spiritually enriching as it is materially rewarding.

A Ritualistic Approach

Approaching this balance ritualistically involves not just spells for material gain, but also practices that keep you grounded spiritually. It's a dance of lighting candles for prosperity while also meditating on gratitude and the non-material blessings in your life. It's the art of asking for abundance while also seeking wisdom on how to use that abundance for your spiritual growth and the greater good.

Remember that the quest for wealth in magik is not just a pursuit of money and possessions. It's a deeper exploration of what wealth truly means, how it impacts your spiritual journey, and how you can balance the material with the ethereal. It's about understanding that true prosperity comes from harmonizing the physical comforts with spiritual well-being. Let's tread this path with an open mind and a heart ready to embrace the true essence of wealth in all its forms.

Let's first look at some simple money drawing spells.

MONEY DRAW SPELLS

Spell 1: The Satanic Coin Attraction Spell

Items Needed:

1. Five Copper Coins (US pennies, or similar)

2. Green Candle

3. Patchouli Oil

4. Satan Wealth Sigil

Steps:

1. Anoint the green candle with patchouli oil, symbolizing the drawing of wealth.

2. Arrange the copper coins around the candle in a pentagram shape, connecting them to the earth element and material gain.

3. Place the Satanic Sigil for Wealth in the center of the pentagram.

4. Light the candle and focus on the flame, visualizing the energy of Satan in his Wealth Aspect flowing towards you.

5. Chant the following: "By the power of Satan, wealth flow to me, as I will, so it shall be."

6. Allow the candle to burn completely. Once done, carry the coins with you to attract money.

Spell 2: Satanic Prosperity Jar

Items Needed:

1. Small Jar

2. Green Ribbon

3. Cinnamon Sticks

4. Basil Leaves

5. Satan Wealth Sigil

Steps:

1. Fill the jar with cinnamon sticks and basil leaves, herbs associated with wealth and prosperity.

2. Place the Sigil on top of the herbs.

3. Seal the jar and tie it with the green ribbon, symbolizing the growth and accumulation of wealth.

4. Hold the jar in your hands and visualize Satan's Wealth Aspect energizing the contents.

5. Keep the jar in your home or workplace to draw in prosperity and abundance.

Spell 3: Satanic Money Flow Visualization

Items Needed:

1. **Gold Candle**

2. **Sandalwood Incense**

3. **Small Mirror**

4. **Picture or Symbol Representing Wealth**

Steps:

1. Light the sandalwood incense to cleanse your space and attract positive energies.

2. Place the gold candle in front of the mirror, signifying wealth being reflected back to you.

3. Put the picture or symbol of wealth behind the candle, visible in the mirror.

4. Light the candle, focusing on the reflection, and visualize the flow of money coming towards you.

5. Recite: "Through Satan's guidance, wealth is mine, in abundance, through the divine."

6. Meditate on the flame for a few minutes, cementing the image of wealth flowing to you.

7. Extinguish the candle and thank Satan for his Wealth Aspect's influence.

Each of these spells utilizes Satan's energy in his Wealth Aspect, focusing on attracting and manifesting prosperity and financial abundance in your life. Remember to approach these spells with a clear mind and focused intent for the best outcomes.

RITUAL FOR LONG-TERM INCREASE IN INCOME WITH SATAN

This ritual focuses on invoking Satan for a sustained increase in income over many years. It is designed to align your energies with the forces of abundance and prosperity, channeling them into your financial life for enduring stability and growth.

The request or petition should be worded specifically, making sure there are no loopholes or possibility of the magik harming anyone. The gold candle needs to be in a sturdy holder, as the requests paper is placed under it, and the candle burns completely. We'll be using the Wealth sigil and Satan's Material Mastery summoning.

Items Needed:

A black altar cloth

Altar candles, black and red

One large gold candle (representing wealth)

Frankincense incense (for purification and spiritual connection)

A small bowl of soil (symbolizing grounding and growth)

A piece of paper and a pen

Seven small coins (symbolizing incoming wealth)

Satan's Wealth Sigil

Offering of expensive wine or whiskey

Actions:

Begin by setting up your sacred space. Lay the black cloth on your altar, representing the vast unknown from which all potential emerges.

Cast a circle using the method you prefer.

Place the gold candle in the center of the altar. This candle is the beacon of your intent, symbolizing the wealth you seek to attract.

Surround the base of the candle with the seven coins, each coin representing an avenue or source through which wealth might flow to you.

Light the frankincense incense, allowing its purifying smoke to cleanse your space and create a bridge between the material and spiritual worlds.

Hold the bowl of soil in your hands, feeling its grounding energy. Place it on the altar as a symbol of your intention to grow your income from a stable foundation.

Write your specific intention for a financial increase on the piece of paper. Be as clear and detailed as possible. Fold the paper and place it under the gold candle's holder.

Summon Satan by saying the following:

> *Renich uberace ninan vesa Ave Satanis!*
>
> *I summon you, Lord Satan!*
>
> *Master of wealth!*
>
> *Renich uberace ninan vesa Ave Satanis!*
>
> *Be with me this day/night*
>
> *Join with me in my space!*
>
> *Renich uberace ninan vesa Ave Satanis!*

Light the gold candle while focusing intently on your desire for increased income. As the flame ignites, imagine it lighting up pathways to financial prosperity.

Speak aloud your request. Express your desire for a long-term increase in income and ask for Satan's guidance and empowerment in this endeavor. Acknowledge his role in challenging and transforming your financial situation.

Spend a few moments in meditation, visualizing the wealth you desire flowing towards you, creating stability and abundance in your life for years to come.

Close the ritual by thanking Satan for his presence and assistance. Give him the offering by placing the glass holding the wine or whiskey on his Wealth Master Sigil.

As always, say something like this when doing the offering:

Lord Satan! Please accept this humble offering of (what it is) in return for your help on this matter.

Let the gold candle burn down safely.

After 24 hours, dispose of the offering outside, onto bare dirt.

Keep Satan's Wealth Sigil on your altar, alongside the coins, as a reminder of your ongoing magikal work for financial prosperity.

Remember, this ritual is not just a onetime act but the beginning of a long-term magikal journey towards financial stability. Regular reflection on your goals and occasional repetition of the ritual can reinforce your intent and strengthen the magikal energies at work.

RITUAL FOR A WINDFALL OF MONEY

Sometimes, we need a large amount of money, often quickly. As I have said previously, do not wait until it's an emergency to work magik for money. But unexpected emergencies sometime appear, quite suddenly, and we need to take rapid action.

Start with this ritual. Then be prepared to do any physical actions you suddenly need to make, such as going for a walk and perhaps finding money, or finding yourself in a situation where you might meet someone who'll option that book you've been working on, or a potential employer.

This ritual will deliver unexpected money. However, also consider the magik might work to bring you an extra work shift, or a side job earning a lot of extra money. Keep your mind open to the possibilities.

Prior to the ritual, prepare your request or petition like you did for the wealth ritual. Make notes, Word this carefully, as I have previously cautioned.

This ritual ends a bit differently. You'll need to be ready to distribute the energized coins around your house/apartment as instructed at the end of the ritual.

Items Needed:

    Altar candles

    Ritual Candle in Gold or Green

    Heavy duty candle holder for the ritual candle.

    Incense (I use frankincense)

    Satan's Wealth Sigil

    Six coins, of any size

    Offering of wine or whiskey

Actions:

    Prepare your altar in any way you see fit.

Light the frankincense incense, allowing its purifying smoke to cleanse your space and create a bridge between the material and spiritual worlds.

Light the candles, except for the ritual specific gold candle.

Write your specific intention for a financial windfall on the piece of paper. Be as clear and detailed as possible.

Room lights out.

Cast a circle using your favorite method. We're calling on the same aspect of Satan as in the previous ritual.

Say

Renich uberace ninan vesa Ave Satanis!

I summon you, Lord Satan!

Master of wealth!

Renich uberace ninan vesa Ave Satanis

Be with me this day/night

Join with me in my space!

Renich uberace ninan vesa Ave Satanis

Money now comes to me,

From unexpected sources, in ever-increasing amounts,

In a safe manner, harming none.

At this point, pick up your written intention and say it out loud.

Fold the paper as small as you can make it, and place it next to the gold candle. Hold your hands out over the candle, and say:

Lord Satan! I ask now that you energize and bless this candle to bring me a large windfall of money.

Now, light the candle. Hold your hands over the folded paper and recite:

Into these words, my intention, I now direct great power, power to manifest my desire, power drawn from within me, and power from Lord Satan.

Pause a moment, with your hand still out, and visualize golden energy glowing around your hands, which now bloom and enter the paper with your intention.

Next, pick up the coins. Holding them in your hand, again visualize this golden light. Hold this visual for as long as you can, at least 30 seconds.

Now say: *Lord Satan, please enchant these coins to draw money to me in great amounts!*

Pick up the wine or whiskey, pour a small amount into a small glass, and hold it up. Say:

Lord Satan, please accept this humble offering of (the offering) in gratitude for acting upon my request.

The ritual is done at this point.

Gather up the coins, and go outside. Hide or bury them at all four corners of your property, or hide them inside the far corners of an apartment. Then, hide or bury one coin at the start of the path to your front door, then hide or bury the last coin under the threshold of the front door.

This activates the coins to draw money to you.

I have done this one a number of times and it typically works within a week.

FAQ:

Does the currency of the coins count? *No, they can be coins foreign to you, or of any money amount. Use small dimes for the easiest to hide, or larger coins. This is your choice.*

I don't have access to the soil around my condo/apartment, what do I do? *Hide the coins inside. Go* *to each corner and hide the coins under something, like inside a planter, edges of the carpet, tape it to the corner using any tape.*

I can't access the main walk way to my door, it's all concrete or ...ect. *Do the best you can. I've hidden small coins in the expansion gaps in concrete, or along the edge of the sidewalk.*

How do I hide the coin under my door's threshold? *Easy enough. You can tape the coin along the edge of the door itself.*

What if someone finds the coins? Will this stop the magik? *I have found, even in the most heavily traveled areas, the coins will stay hidden, especially the ones on the walkway to your door, for quite a while.*

This magik uses the energy of the earth to funnel money to you. Once you've gotten your windfall, or if the ritual might not be working, gather up the hidden coins, wash in salt water to cleanse them, then run the ritual again.

CHAPTER 7

CONTROLLING AND INFLUENCING PEOPLE

This type of ritual and power can be used to not only obtain that crucial promotion at work, but to also sway someone into your arms if a standard love ritual doesn't seem to work.

Do be advised: The love/sex aspect of this magik may be short-lived. If you wish a long-term relationship with a target - I urge you to reconsider going this route and instead work the rituals in the Love Magik chapter. Although using the power to secure a temporary lover, it might backfire and make your life worse.

You have been warned.

In the following material, I'll look at general control and influence. The rituals can be easily modified for most any situation.

The Role of Satan in Control and Influence Magik

Within the landscape of magikal practice, Satan is commonly seen as the personification of personal empowerment, acting as a catalyst for change and a proficient manipulator. The act of seeking his assistance for control and influence is more than just harnessing a dark, external force, practitioners are doing much more.

Before embarking on any ritual aimed at influencing or controlling others, it's paramount to anchor oneself in ethical awareness. Magik, like any potent tool, comes with a responsibility to use it wisely and harmlessly. The practitioner must always consider the potential impact of their actions on others' free will and autonomy. It's like walking a tightrope; one must constantly balance personal desires with the ethical implications of influencing another's path.

Rituals for controlling and influencing people in magik are nuanced and require a delicate balance between intent, ethical practice, and the natural laws of the universe. While these rituals can be powerful tools in achieving personal and professional goals, they must be approached with respect, caution, and a clear understanding of their potential impact. By focusing on enhancing personal attributes like charisma and communication skills, practitioners can influence situations positively without compromising the autonomy and free will of others.

THE ETHICAL LABYRINTH OF CONTROL MAGIK

This magik, the art of controlling and influencing people, occupies a controversial niche. This section peers into the murky waters of ethics surrounding these practices, particularly when invoking a figure as potent and complex as Satan. The exploration here is not just about the 'how' but significantly about the 'should we' of control and influence magik.

At the heart of control and influence magik lies an ethical labyrinth that challenges even the most seasoned practitioners. The notion of bending another's will or swaying their decisions through magikal means is fraught with moral implications. It raises profound questions about free will, consent, and the karmic repercussions of using occult powers to influence another's path. Just thought I'd get that out of the way right now.

Navigating this labyrinth requires a keen understanding of ethical boundaries. It's akin to walking a tightrope where one misstep could lead to unintended consequences. The practitioner must constantly balance their desires with the moral responsibility of respecting others' autonomy. It's a dance with shadows where the lines between influence and manipulation are as thin as a spider's silk.

Invoking Satan for Influence: Power and Responsibility

Invoking Satan for influence and power is a journey that intertwines esoteric wisdom with profound moral introspection. In many spiritual traditions, Satan is not merely a symbol of defiance and strength, but also a beacon of wisdom and enlightenment. When one turns to Satan for control and influence magik, they are not simply seeking to harness a rebellious force; they are aligning with a profound ally, one that offers deep insights into the intricacies of human will and psychology.

Engaging with Satan in the context of influence magik requires more than just the utterance of spells or the performance of rituals. It involves an intricate dance with a force that embodies multifaceted aspects of existence. Satan, in this respect, represents the duality of light and shadow within the human psyche. He is the whisperer of hidden knowledge, the revealer of harsh truths, and the guide through the labyrinth of human motivations.

The Thin Veil Between Influence and Coercion

One of the key ethical challenges in control and influence magik is distinguishing between benign influence and outright coercion. This distinction is crucial, for while influencing someone might involve guiding or persuading, coercion strips the individual of their free will. The practitioner must ask themselves: "Am I guiding someone towards a path for their betterment, or am I imposing my will upon them?"

This is important: For true, lasting effect, this has to be more of a gentle guiding, versus imposing your will. Sure, some of you may wish to impose your will, but the effects will be a lot longer lasting if you act as more of a guide, and less of a master.

The Ripple Effect on Relationships

Engaging in control and influence magik can have a ripple effect on the practitioner's personal relationships. It can lead to a loss of trust and authenticity in connections. It's like playing a game where the other players are unaware of the rules or even that they are playing. This deception can lead to a hollow victory, where the external gains are overshadowed by internal loss.

While these rituals offer powerful tools, they come with a caveat - a reminder to tread carefully, respecting the free will and autonomy of others. The journey through this aspect of magik is not just about wielding power, but also about understanding its weight and learning to use it with wisdom and responsibility.

THE CHARISMA RITUAL

One of the more subtle forms of influence in magikal practice is the Charisma Ritual. This ritual doesn't aim to control or manipulate in the traditional sense. Instead, it's designed to enhance the practitioner's natural charm and persuasive abilities, making them more effective in social interactions.

Preparing your petition is the start of the magik. Using a standard pen and some decent paper, write out your intention. Be clear, concise, and include phrases like "I speak with clarity and charm" or "My words flow effortlessly and attract positive attention."

You can use this example: "Lord Satan! I ask that you assist me in become more charismatic! My words flow effortlessly and attract positive attention. People respond to my every word, and I speak easily, and without hesitation." Or words to this effect.

Craft a sigil of this statement. Shorten it, like this example: "Lord Satan, grant me effortless charisma and persuasive speech that captivates and influences effortlessly." Use my online tutorial on sigil creation (see appendix) and turn this into an effective sigil.

Items needed:

Altar cloth, in blue, or basic black

Altar candles - black and red.

Ritual candle in blue

Incense - Frankincense or Dragon Blood, or a mix.

A peacock's feather for charisma*

Honey or brown sugar to "sweeten your words"

Satan's Material Master Sigil

Sigil of charisma if you made one

Offering to Satan of a single glass of spirits, such as vodka or whiskey.

(Optional: Athame, crystals, goblet of water.)

The Ritual:

To begin, light the incense, then light the altar's candle. Turn out the room's lights.

Cast a secure circle (of your own choosing) and then get ready for the ritual.

When ready, say:

Renich uberace ninan vesa Ave Satanis

Renich uberace ninan vesa Ave Satanis!

Renich uberace ninan vesa Ave Satanis!

Lord Satan, I ask now that you join with me in my space

I ask that you lend me your ears, and grant me this boon!

Pause a moment, and observe the incense smoke and candle flames for the subtle indications Satan is with you in your space.

At this time, read your petition that you have prepared.

Now, visualize yourself in various social situations, where you are communicating effectively and influencing others positively with your charisma. Take your time with this. This is a key component, so take your time and make the images as real as possible.

If you have created a specific sigil for this, pick it up now, and say: *"Lord Satan, I ask that you activate this sigil to bring me charisma. While I keep this sigil, the magik continues!"*

Pick up the offering, and hold it up. Say:

"Lord Satan, please accept this humble offering of (whiskey or whatever). I hereby give this over to you as thanks for acting on my petition!"

Time to close the ritual.

This is done my simply announcing that the ritual is done.

Allow the offering to stay on Satan's sigil until the next day, then pour it out onto the ground outside.

You are done.

Precautions and Select Targeting

When performing rituals to influence others, it's crucial to be selective and precise in targeting. The practitioner should avoid broad, undefined intentions, as these can lead to unintended consequences. For instance, influencing a specific person for a constructive purpose, such as encouraging a friend to overcome their fears, is more focused and less ethically ambiguous than attempting to sway a large group for personal gain.

RITUAL OF COMPELLING

This is a powerful ritual. The magik might be fleeting, for no matter how powerful your magik, compelling magik has a limited time that is actually works. A good time to work this is when you are negotiating for a contract or job, or in any situation where you need subtle, and firm, control over another person.

This ritual demands a blood offering and uses the Egregore aspect of Satan.

Craft a statement that might read like: "Lord Satan! I ask that you control this person ____(name)__, that I now exert control over them for the purpose of _____. I ask that this be done gently, but firmly. This magik will last for longer than (time limit)."

Setting a time limit will act to negate the ritual if you no longer wish this person to be under your control. Know this - the magik will naturally dissipate within 2 lunar cycles if a time limit isn't already set. Use lunar timing for this - such as "until the next full moon."

Other items you'll need is a clear photo of the target, and their name written on the back in red ink. I use a "sharpie" marker for this.

Take your time on this, all while understanding this magik does work, and works well.

Items Needed:
    Altar cloth, in blue, or basic black
    Altar candles - black and red.
    Ritual candle in blue
    Incense
    A peacock's feather for charisma*
    Honey or brown sugar to "sweeten your words"
    Satan's Egregore Sigil (two copies)
    Diabetic lancet and fire proof bowl
    (Optional: Athame, crystals, goblet of water.)

The Ritual:

To begin, light the incense, then light the altar's candle. Turn out the room's lights.

Cast a secure circle (of your own choosing) and then get ready for the ritual.

When ready, say:

    Tasa reme laris Satan, Ave Satanis!

    Tasa reme laris Satan, Ave Satanis!

    Tasa reme laris Satan, Ave Satanis!

    Lord Satan, I ask now that you join with me in my space

    I ask that you lend me your ears, and grant me this boon!

Pause a moment, and observe the incense smoke and candle flames for the subtle indications Satan is with you in your space.

At this time, read your petition that you have prepared.

Next, visualize yourself the desired results. Take your time with this. This is a key component, so take your time and make the images as real as possible.

If you have created a specific sigil for this, pick it up now, and say: ***"Lord Satan, I ask that you activate this sigil to bring me (target's name). While I keep this sigil, the magik continues!"***

Pick up the small sigil, then prick a finger (any finger, it doesn't matter) and place a single drop of blood onto the sigil. Then touch a corner of the sigil to a candle flame (ANY candle) and say:

"Lord Satan, please accept this humble offering of my essence. I hereby give this over to you as thanks for acting on my petition!"

Time to close the ritual.

This is done my simply announcing that the ritual is done.

Allow the offering to stay on Satan's sigil until the next day, then pour it out onto the ground outside.

You are done.

CHAPTER 8

HEALING AND PROTECTION MAGIK

The figure of Satan stands as a paradox, embodying not just rebellion and power but also harboring unexpected benevolence, particularly in the areas of healing and protection. This section aims to illuminate the less-explored, yet profoundly compassionate aspects of working with Satan, challenging the conventional portrayal and revealing a figure of deep, multifaceted potential.

The Unconventional Healer: Satan's Role in Restoration and Balance

The concept of Satan as a healer might initially seem incongruous. Traditionally seen as a symbol of temptation and chaos, Satan, in a more nuanced view, also holds the keys to profound knowledge and understanding of the human condition. This includes an innate understanding of healing, not just of the body, but of the mind and spirit.

Why Satan, one might ask? The answer lies in the very attributes that make Satan an enigmatic figure. Satan, representing the ultimate rebel, inherently understands the struggles, pain, and ailments that can afflict humankind. In magik, this understanding is transformed into a potent tool for healing. Satan's energy is directed not towards destruction but towards the restoration of balance and harmony within the self.

Healing takes quite a bit of positive energy flowing to the target person. Satan is as powerful as any spirit in the astral (and beyond). I have used him for this on three occasions, each time with impressive results.

The Protector in the Shadows: Satan's Shielding Power

In protection magik, Satan emerges as a formidable guardian. Often misconceived as a force to be guarded against, Satan, in fact, can be a powerful ally in shielding oneself from harm. This role as a protector stem from his deep connection to the more profound, often darker aspects of life and the universe.

Invoking Satan for protection involves tapping into this profound wellspring of power. It's an acknowledgment that understanding darkness is essential to combat it. Satan, as a protector, offers not just defense against external threats but also a strengthening of one's inner fortitude, creating an impenetrable shield forged from awareness and understanding.

Healing and Protection: The Synergy of Knowledge and Power

The interplay of healing and protection in working with Satan is a dance of knowledge and power. On the one hand, Satan offers insight into the mysteries of healing – understanding the hidden ailments that plague the soul and the remedies that can restore wholeness. On the other, he provides the strength and resilience needed to create barriers against harm, both physical and spiritual.

In magik, working with Satan in these areas is not a passive act. It requires active engagement with the forces at play, a deep introspection into one's own needs and vulnerabilities, and a willingness to embrace the unconventional paths that Satan's guidance may reveal.

Exploring the benevolent aspects of working with Satan in healing and protection magik opens a gateway to a deeper understanding of this complex figure. It challenges practitioners to look beyond the surface, to find healing and safeguarding in what might initially appear shadowy or daunting. This journey with Satan, far from being a descent into darkness, is an ascent into a more profound understanding of balance, restoration, and the protective powers hidden in the unseen corners of the universe.

THE HEALING POWER OF SATAN'S MAGIK

In our occult world, where the lines between light and dark are often blurred, lies the potent and multifaceted magik of Satan. Traditionally viewed through a lens of fear and misunderstanding, Satan's magik is, in fact, an incredibly powerful force that can be harnessed for a variety of purposes, including healing. This section explores how the intense and dynamic energy of Satan can be channeled into a tool for profound healing.

The Versatile Nature of Satanic Magik

Satanic magik presents itself as an extraordinarily adaptable force, one that seamlessly aligns with the intentions and desires of the practitioner. This form of magik transcends traditional boundaries and simplistic classifications of good and evil. It embodies a dynamic and malleable essence, allowing for a wide spectrum of applications and manifestations, all contingent on the practitioner's will and purpose.

Adaptability and Fluidity

Satanic magik is akin to a chameleon in its ability to adapt and transform. Just as a chameleon alters its color to match its surroundings, Satanic magik shifts in response to the practitioner's intentions and goals. This quality makes it a uniquely responsive and potent form of magik, capable of serving diverse purposes and achieving varied outcomes.

One of the most striking aspects of Satanic magik is its defiance of the conventional binary of good and evil. It operates outside the traditional moral frameworks, challenging practitioners to approach it with an open mind, free from the constraints of conventional moral dogma. This magik invites a deeper exploration of ethical complexities, encouraging a more nuanced understanding of morality and intent.

Healing Magik

When directed towards healing, Satanic magik becomes a powerful tool for restoration and rejuvenation. It channels energies that can be used to mend, to heal, and to restore balance. This aspect of Satanic magik is particularly significant, as it underscores the potential for what is often perceived as a dark or malevolent force to be used for positive, life-affirming purposes.

Utilizing Satanic magik for healing purposes requires the practitioner to look beyond entrenched beliefs and preconceived notions. It demands an open-minded approach, one that acknowledges the multifaceted nature of magik and its capacity to effect change in various forms. This challenges practitioners to expand their understanding of magik, seeing it not just as a tool for personal gain or power but as a means of contributing to the greater good.

The versatile nature of Satanic magik makes it a profoundly effective and transformative force in the hands of a skilled practitioner. Its ability to adapt to the practitioner's will, to serve purposes that defy traditional moral categorizations, and to act as a conduit for healing and restoration, highlights the complex and multifaceted nature of this magikal practice. Satanic magik, in its essence, is a testament to the power of intention and the potential of magik to transcend conventional boundaries, offering a path to both personal and communal transformation.

Harnessing the Energy for Healing

The key to utilizing Satan's magik for healing lies in the strength and clarity of one's intention. It requires a focused mind and a clear vision of the desired outcome. Whether it's physical healing, emotional restoration, or spiritual balance, the practitioner must align their will with the potent energies at their command.

Utilizing specific rituals and incantations, the practitioner can direct the formidable energy of Satan towards the act of healing. These rituals often involve calling upon Satan not as a malevolent force, but as a source of strength and transformation. Incantations, charged with the practitioner's intent, act as a bridge between the physical and the ethereal, channeling the energy where it is needed.

In these rituals, symbolic items play a crucial role. Items such as candles, crystals, and herbs, each chosen for their alignment with healing properties, become vessels for Satan's energy. They are charged with the magikal intent and become physical representations of the healing process.

The Ethics of Healing with Satan's Magik

While the power of Satan's magik is vast and versatile, it comes with an ethical responsibility. The practitioner must constantly evaluate their motives and the potential impact of their work. Healing magik, particularly when it involves such a powerful entity, should always be performed with the highest good in mind, respecting the natural laws and the autonomy of those being healed.

Exploring the healing aspects of Satan's magik opens up a new dimension in the practice of the occult arts. It invites the practitioner to step into a world where power and intent intertwine, where the energies of a traditionally dark figure can be transformed into a beacon of healing and restoration. This journey is not just about the physical act of healing, but also about personal growth, understanding, and the breaking of boundaries that have long confined the true potential of magikal practice.

Types of Rituals for Self-Healing, Protection, and Empowerment

In the grand theater of Satan-centric magik, the rituals for self-healing, protection, and empowerment stand as powerful acts, each a testament to the multifaceted nature of this enigmatic figure. These rituals, steeped in ancient wisdom and adapted for modern practitioners, offer a pathway to harness the potent energies associated with Satan for personal betterment and safeguarding.

The Art of Self-Healing

Think about a garden overgrown with weeds, its beauty obscured, its potential unfulfilled. This garden is akin to the human soul when burdened with emotional and spiritual maladies. Self-healing rituals in Satan-centric magik are akin to the careful, deliberate act of tending to this garden, removing the weeds, and nurturing the plants back to health. These rituals often involve a deep introspection, a journey into the innermost recesses of the self. They may include practices such as candle magik, where specific colors are chosen for their healing properties, or the crafting of talismans that serve as focal points for healing energies. The invocation of Satan in these rituals is not a call to a malevolent force, but rather a summoning of inner strength, resilience, and the power to heal oneself.

Protection Magik: A Shield Against the Storm

In the practice of High Magik, and indeed across various forms of magik, protection rituals are fundamental. These rituals can be visualized as the crafting of a mystical shield, a formidable barrier designed to ward off negative forces and energies that one may encounter in their spiritual journey. When these rituals are conducted in alignment with Satan, they acquire an intensified potency, drawing upon his formidable energy to fortify and safeguard the practitioner.

The core of protection magik lies in the creation of a metaphysical shield. This is not a physical construct but an energetic one, envisioned and brought into being through focused intent and ritualistic practice. It serves as a bastion against external negative influences, whether they be malevolent spirits, harmful energies, or psychic attacks. One I teach in my coaching sessions is generating a metallic energy barrier. Using Satan's energy as well as your own, this barrier is impervious.

By invoking Satan in these protective practices, the practitioner taps into a potent source of power. Satan, as a symbol and force in High Magik, represents strength, resilience, and defiance. Utilizing this energy in protection magik amplifies the effectiveness of the rituals, creating a more robust and impenetrable shield.

One of the fundamental practices in protection magik is the casting of protective circles. These circles act as physical and spiritual boundaries, sanctifying the space within as safe and secure. The act of casting a circle often involves recitations, the use of ritual tools, and the visualization of protective energy forming a barrier around the practitioner.

The use of sigils and symbols plays a significant role in protection magik. These symbols, which may include pentagrams, hexagrams, or personalized sigils, are believed to hold defensive power. They can be drawn, visualized, or created as physical objects to enhance the protective energy of a space or person.

The creation of herbal mixtures and amulets is another aspect of protection magik. These may include herbs known for their protective properties, such as sage, rosemary, or mugwort. Combined and carried as amulets or used in ritual burning, these herbal mixtures serve as tangible manifestations of protective intent.

The practices within protection magik are deeply rooted in the belief that the energies and forces we interact with have a tangible impact on our wellbeing. This belief extends beyond mere superstition, intertwining with the principles of energy manipulation and psychic defense that are central to many magikal practices. Protection magik, particularly when aligned with the powerful energies associated with Satan, is a vital component of a practitioner's repertoire, offering a means to maintain spiritual integrity and personal safety in the face of various metaphysical challenges.

So, you see, protection magik in High Magik is a sophisticated and multi-faceted practice, blending ritual, symbolism, and the harnessing of powerful energies. It underscores the importance of safeguarding oneself against negative influences and emphasizes the potent role that Satanic energy can play in bolstering these protective measures.

Empowerment Rituals: Tapping into Inner Power

Empowerment rituals in Satan-centric magik are akin to standing atop a mountain, drawing strength from the earth below and the skies above. These rituals are designed to tap into the wellspring of personal power, often lying dormant within. They may involve meditative practices that focus on connecting with the energy of Satan as a source of empowerment, or the use of chants and mantras that affirm one's strength and capabilities. These rituals are a celebration of the self, a recognition of one's own power and potential, and a call to manifest this power in the physical world.

Together, these rituals form a symphony of magikal practice, each note resonating with a different aspect of the human experience – healing, protection, and empowerment. They represent a journey not just into the realm of Satan-centric magik but into the depths of one's own soul. It's a path that requires courage, for it involves confronting one's own shadows and fears, but it's also a journey that promises transformation and enlightenment.

Let's now move on to the magik, remembering that each practice is not just a set of steps to be followed but an art to be mastered. They require not just knowledge and skill but also intuition, creativity, and a deep connection with the energies at play. Approaching these rituals with respect, understanding, and an open heart will unlock their true potential, guiding the practitioner on a transformative journey of healing, protection, and empowerment.

SPELLS FOR HEALING AND PROTECTION

Spell 1: Satanic Shield of Protection

Items Needed:
1. Black Candle
2. Salt

3. Satan's Benevolent Sigil

Steps:
1. Light the black candle to symbolize the absorption of negative energies.
2. Draw a circle around yourself with salt, creating a physical and spiritual barrier.
3. Place the Satanic Sigil within your circle as a focal point for protective energy.
4. Visualize a shield of light emanating from the sigil, enveloping you in a protective field.
5. Recite: "By Satan's benevolent shield, I am protected, I am healed."
6. Maintain this visualization for a few minutes, feeling the protective energy solidify around you.
7. Extinguish the candle and carry a bit of the salt with you for ongoing protection.

Spell 2: Satanic Aura of Safeguarding

Items Needed:
1. Lavender Incense
2. Small Quartz Crystal
3. Piece of Paper with Satan's Benevolent Protector Sigil

Steps:
1. Light the lavender incense to purify the space and invite calming energies.
2. Hold the quartz crystal, a natural amplifier, in your hand.
3. Place the paper with the Satanic sigil in front of you.

4. Focus on the sigil and crystal, and visualize a soothing, protective aura growing around you.

5. Whisper: "Satan's energy shields me, in safety and peace, I shall be."

6. Carry the crystal with you as a physical reminder of your protective aura.

Spell 3: Satanic Guardian Circle

Items Needed:
1. Four White Candles
2. Sandalwood Oil
3. Satan's Benevolent Protector Sigil

Steps:
1. Anoint each white candle with sandalwood oil for purification and protection.

2. Arrange the candles in a square around you, each representing a cardinal direction.

3. Place the image of the Satanic sigil in the center.

4. Light each candle, starting with the north, and moving clockwise.

5. As you light each candle, envision a wall of protective energy rising from the flames.

6. Stand or sit in the center and say: "Protected by Satan's grace, in this circle, I find my safe space."

7. Spend a few moments in the center of your guardian circle, feeling the protective energies.

8. Extinguish the candles, knowing the protective energy remains with you.

Each of these spells leverages the energy of Satan in his Benevolent Protector & Healing Aspect, creating a protective field around you. These rituals are simple yet powerful ways to harness Satanic energy for personal protection and peace of mind.

RITUAL FOR THE ART OF SELF-HEALING

This ritual taps into the transformative and healing energies associated with Satan, focusing on personal healing and rejuvenation. The steps are designed to guide you, my reader, through a process of inner healing and renewal.

Items Needed:

Altar candles in white

Black Candle: Symbolizes absorption of negative energies and the power of transformation.

Red Candle: Represents vitality, health, and life force.

A Bowl of Saltwater: For purification and emotional cleansing.

Healing Crystals: Such as amethyst or quartz, to enhance healing energies.

Incense (preferably frankincense or myrrh): For purifying the space and facilitating a connection with higher energies.

A piece of Paper and Pen: To write down aspects of yourself that need healing.

Satan's Benevolent Protector Aspect sigil

Offering of flowers, or wine

Actions:

Begin, as always, by lighting the altar candles, the white candles only. Then the incense. Room lights off.

Next, cast a protective circle using the saltwater, sprinkling it around your space while visualizing a barrier of light that safeguards you from any negative influences. Or you may use any of the other circles I list in this book.

Lighting the Candles: This ritual has a unique candle lighting sequence. Start by lighting just the black candle, acknowledging its power to absorb negativity and transform energies. Then light the red candle, focusing on its ability to invigorate and promote healing.

Take the paper and pen and write down specific aspects of yourself that you wish to heal. This could be physical ailments, emotional wounds, or mental stress.

With your intentions clearly written, invoke Satan with the following words:

Ayer Ganen Tepar Va Satanis!

Ayer Ganen Tepar Va Satanis!

Ayer Ganen Tepar Va Satanis!

Satan, guide of transformation and renewal,

I seek your aid in my journey of healing.

Empower me to absorb and transmute my afflictions,

Replacing them with vitality and strength.

Hold the healing crystals and enter a meditative state. Visualize the energies of the candles interacting, where the black candle absorbs and transmutes your written afflictions, and the red candle infuses you with health and vigor.

Affirmation of Healing: Repeat affirmations that align with your healing intentions, such as *"I am whole, healthy, and rejuvenated by the transformative power within me."*

After your meditation, offer gratitude to Satan for the guidance, and energy provided in your healing process. Pick up the offering and place it near Satan's sigil. Then say:

Lord Satan! Please accept this humble offering of (item or offering) in gratitude for your help in this matter!

Extinguish the candles, formally close the circle by thanking the protective energies, and dispose of the paper in a way that symbolizes release – such as burying it or burning it safely.

After 24 hours, dispose of the offering by placing it into nature or (with wine) pouring it on the ground.

After the ritual, engage in self-care activities that align with your healing process, like a warm bath, restful sleep, or nourishing food.

This ritual is a powerful tool in the art of self-healing, combining the transformative energies associated with Satan with the practitioner's intent and actions. Regular practice can enhance personal healing and contribute to overall well-being.

RITUAL FOR HEALTHY WEIGHT LOSS

This ritual taps into the transformative and healing energies associated with Satan, focusing on personal healing and rejuvenation. The steps are designed to guide you, my reader, through a process of inner healing and renewal.

Items Needed:

Altar candles in white

Black Candle: Symbolizes absorption of negative energies and the power of transformation.

Red Candle: Represents vitality, health, and life force.

A Bowl of Saltwater: For purification and emotional cleansing.

Healing Crystals: Such as amethyst or quartz, to enhance healing energies.

Incense (preferably frankincense or myrrh): For purifying the space and facilitating a connection with higher energies.

A piece of Paper and Pen: To write down your goals of achieving a healthy weight and lifestyle.

Satan's Healing Aspect sigil

Offering of flowers, or wine

Actions:

Begin, as always, by lighting the altar candles, the white candles only. Then the incense. Room lights off.

Next, cast a protective circle using the saltwater, sprinkling it around your space while visualizing a barrier of light that safeguards you from any negative influences. Or you may use any of the other circles I list in this book.

Lighting the Candles: This ritual has a unique candle lighting sequence. Star by lighting just the black candle, acknowledging its power to absorb negativity and transform energies. Then light the red candle, focusing on its ability to invigorate and promote healing.

Take the paper and pen and write down specific aspects of yourself that you wish to heal. This could be physical ailments, emotional wounds, or mental stress.

With your intentions clearly written, invoke Satan with the following words:

Ayer Ganen Tepar Va Satanis!

Ayer Ganen Tepar Va Satanis!

Ayer Ganen Tepar Va Satanis!

Satan, guide of transformation and renewal,

I seek your aid in my journey of healing.

I ask that I be aligned with my perfect weight,

Empower me to lose weight safely and easily,

Restore my vitality and strength.

Hold the healing crystals and enter a meditative state. Visualize the energies of the candles interacting, where the black candle absorbs and transmutes your written afflictions, and the red candle infuses you with health and vigor.

Affirmation of Healing: Repeat affirmations that align with your healing intentions, such as *"I am whole, healthy, and rejuvenated by the transformative power within me."*

After your meditation, offer gratitude to Satan for the guidance, and energy provided in your healing process. Pick up the offering and place it near Satan's sigil. Then say:

Lord Satan! Please accept this humble offering of (item or offering) in gratitude for your help in this matter!

Extinguish the candles, formally close the circle by thanking the protective energies, and dispose of the paper in a way that symbolizes release – such as burying it or burning it safely.

After 24 hours, dispose of the offering by placing it into nature or (with wine) pouring it on the ground.

After the ritual, engage in self-care activities that align with your healing process, like a warm bath, restful sleep, or nourishing food.

This ritual is a powerful tool in the art of self-healing, combining the transformative energies associated with Satan with the practitioner's intent and actions. Regular practice can enhance personal healing and contribute to overall well-being.

RITUAL FOR THE ART OF HEALING ANOTHER

This ritual focuses on harnessing the energies associated with Satan for the purpose of healing another person. It is a sacred process that requires respect, compassion, and a deep understanding of the energies involved.

Items Needed:

Two White Candles: Symbolizing purity and the positive energy of healing.

A Photograph or Personal Item of the Person to be Healed: To create a connection with them.

Healing Crystals (such as Rose Quartz or Green Aventurine): Known for their properties of healing and nurturing.

Incense (preferably lavender or sandalwood): For cleansing and creating a calming atmosphere.

A Small Bowl of Water: Representing emotional healing and clarity.

A Piece of Paper and Pen: To write down the healing intentions.

Photograph and name for targeted healing

Satan's Sigil of Healing and Protection

Offering of wine or sweet breads

Actions:

Cast a circle using your favorite method.

Position the two white candles on either side of the photograph or personal item of the person who needs healing.

Light the incense and then light the candles, focusing on the intent to channel healing energy.

Hold the photograph or personal item and take a moment to connect with the person's energy. Visualize them in your mind, healthy and whole.

On the piece of paper, write down specific intentions or wishes for the person's healing. Be clear and focused in your intent.

With the intentions set, invoke Satan with the following words:

Ayer Ganen Tepar Va Satanis!

Ayer Ganen Tepar Va Satanis!

Ayer Ganen Tepar Va Satanis!

Satan, bearer of enlightenment and transformative power,

I call upon you to channel your healing energies through me

to [person's name].

Guide this process with your wisdom and strength.

Directing Healing Energy: Holding the healing crystals, visualize a stream of healing light emanating from the candles, amplified by the crystals, and directed towards the photograph or personal item. See this light enveloping the person in a soothing, healing glow.

Speak out loud your written healing intentions, affirming each with conviction and belief in their manifestation.

After your meditation, offer gratitude to Satan for the guidance and energy provided in your healing process. Pick up the offering and place it near Satan's sigil. Then say:

Lord Satan! Please accept this humble offering of (item or offering) in gratitude for your help in this matter!

Extinguish the candles, formally close the circle by thanking the protective energies, and dispose of the paper in a way that symbolizes release – such as burying it or burning it safely.

After 24 hours, dispose of the offering by placing it into nature or (with wine) pouring it on the

Follow-Up: Keep the photograph or personal item in a place where you can see it daily, reinforcing your healing intentions until you feel the process is complete.

This ritual is a powerful means of directing healing energy to another person through the guidance and strength of Satan. It combines focused intent with the symbolic power of items and the energies of healing crystals, creating a potent magikal working for the benefit of others.

RITUAL FOR PROTECTION MAGIK

This ritual focuses on invoking Satan's energy for creating a potent shield of protection against negative influences and energies. It is designed to fortify your personal space, acting as a barrier against the storms of negativity you might encounter.

Items Needed:

Black Candle: To absorb and neutralize negative energies.

Protection Stones: Such as black tourmaline or obsidian, known for their grounding and protective qualities.

Salt: For purification and creating protective boundaries.

Incense (preferably sage or cedar): To cleanse the space and ward off negativity.

A Small Mirror: To reflect and repel any negative energies.

A Piece of Paper and Pen: To write down what you wish to protect yourself from.

Actions:

Cleansing the Space: Begin by burning the incense to purify your space. Allow the smoke to waft through the area, envisioning it clearing out all negative energies.

Setting Up Your Protection Items: Place the black candle in the center of your space, surrounded by the protection stones. Place the small mirror behind the candle, facing away from you, to act as a reflector of negativity.

Writing Down Protective Intentions: On the piece of paper, write down specific things or influences you wish to protect yourself from. This act of writing helps to solidify your intentions in our physical reality.

Lighting the Black Candle: Light the candle, visualizing it absorbing all the negativity that might come your way. As you light it, focus on the flame being a source of impenetrable protection.

Salt Circle for Additional Protection: Sprinkle a circle of salt around you, encompassing the candle and stones, while visualizing it forming a barrier that no negative energy can cross.

Invoking Satan for Protection: Say aloud:

Ayer Ganen Tepar Va Satanis!

Ayer Ganen Tepar Va Satanis!

Ayer Ganen Tepar Va Satanis!

Satan, keeper of balance and strength,

I call upon your protective energy.

Shield me from harm and ward off all negativity.

Let this space be sanctified and guarded under your watch.

Visualizing the Protective Shield: Close your eyes and imagine a protective shield emanating from the candle, enveloping you in a bubble of safety. See this shield being fortified by the energy of the protection stones and reflected by the mirror.

Affirm your safety and protection with conviction, stating:

I am surrounded by an unbreakable shield of protection. No harm can penetrate this barrier. I am safe, secure, and shielded.

Thank Satan for his protection and let the candle burn down safely. Keep the stones and mirror in your space as ongoing protective talismans.

Disposing of the Paper: Finally, burn or bury the paper on which you wrote your protective intentions, symbolizing the release of your fears and the activation of your protective magik.

This ritual serves as a powerful tool for creating a magikal barrier against negative influences, harnessing the protective energy of Satan, and grounding and fortifying your personal space. Regular practice can enhance your sense of security and spiritual resilience.

EMPOWERMENT RITUALS: TAPPING INTO INNER POWER

This ritual is designed to help you harness and amplify your inner power, drawing on the energies associated with Satan for empowerment and self-realization.

Items Needed:

Altar Candles (of your choice)

Red Candle: Symbolizing strength, power, and vitality.

Mirror: To reflect your true self and amplify your intentions.

Quartz Crystal: Known for its properties of enhancing energy and intention.

Incense (preferably dragon's blood or cinnamon): To raise energy and enhance personal power.

A Piece of Paper and Pen: To write down the qualities or strengths you wish to amplify.

Satan's Benevolent/Healing Sigil

Offering to Satan of some from nature, a flower, or cream or honey in a small bowl

Actions:

Start by casting the circle of your choice, then begin burning the incense, letting its aroma fill your space. As the smoke rises, envision it clearing away any negativity or doubt.

Light the altar candles, then turn off the room's lights. This helps set the mood for your ritual.

Place the red candle in front of the mirror, ensuring that its reflection is visible. Position the quartz crystal near the base of the candle.

While in the circle, write down the aspects of your personal power you wish to enhance or the qualities you want to embody. This could be confidence, resilience, wisdom, or any other traits you feel will empower you.

Now light the RED candle, focusing on the flame as a beacon of your inner strength and power. Visualize its light growing and enveloping you in its empowering glow.

With your intentions clearly written, invoke Satan with the following words:

Ayer Ganen Tepar Va Satanis!

Ayer Ganen Tepar Va Satanis!

Ayer Ganen Tepar Va Satanis!

I invoke your energy to fortify my inner power.

Amplify my [traits written on the paper],

guiding me to realize my fullest potential.

Meditation and Visualization: Holding the quartz crystal, meditate on the flame and your reflection in the mirror. See yourself embodying the traits you've written down, growing stronger and more empowered. Feel the crystal amplifying your intent and the energy of the ritual.

Affirming Your Power: Repeat affirmations that align with your empowerment goals, such as "I am strong, confident, and empowered by my will and spirit."

Sealing the Ritual: As the ritual comes to a close, visualize the empowered energy solidifying within you, becoming an integral part of your being.

Offering Gratitude and Closing: Thank Satan for the empowerment bestowed upon you.

Pick up the offering, and sit it on Satan's sigil, while saying:

Lord Satan! Please accept this humble offering of (item or offering) in gratitude for your help in this matter!

Extinguish the candle safely.

Dispose of the offering outside.

Post-Ritual Reflection: Keep the piece of paper with your written qualities in a safe place where you can see it daily. Regularly remind yourself of these empowered traits and visualize them continuing to grow within you.

This empowerment ritual is a powerful way to tap into your inner strength and potential, using the energies associated with Satan to boost your confidence and personal power. Regular practice can significantly enhance your sense of self and ability to face life's challenges.

CHAPTER 9

FAME AND CELEBRITY MAGIK - UNDERSTANDING THE PURSUIT OF FAME THROUGH SATAN

In the secretive world of magik, the pursuit of fame and celebrity status presents a unique and intricate path, especially when navigated through the invocation of Satan. This chapter embarks on a journey to understand the conceptual framework of harnessing magikal practices involving Satan in the quest for fame. Here, we probe into the archetype of Satan, not as a mere figure of rebellion and darkness, but as a potent symbol of ambition, power, and the insatiable human desire for recognition.

At the heart of this pursuit lies a fundamental human longing – to be seen, to be acknowledged, and to be remembered. Fame, in its most tantalizing form, offers this and much more. It promises immortality of name, influence over the masses, and a certain kind of power that transcends the ordinary. When one turns to magik, and specifically to Satan, to achieve this, they are tapping into an ancient and primal force. Satan, in this context, emerges not as a harbinger of doom, but as a catalyst for achieving one's highest aspirations in the mortal realm.

Satan, as an archetype, has long been associated with the characteristics of ambition and power. He represents the eternal rebel, challenging the status quo, and pushing the boundaries of what is possible. In the pursuit of fame, these qualities become invaluable. The figure of Satan inspires the practitioner to reach beyond their perceived limits, to dare to dream bigger, and to fiercely chase those dreams. He embodies the raw ambition needed to propel oneself into the limelight and the unyielding power necessary to maintain that position.

Seeking recognition through Satan in magik is a complex dance of aligning one's personal energy with the larger forces at play in the universe. It involves recognizing and harnessing the power within oneself – the power to captivate, to inspire, and to lead. Satan, in this partnership, acts as a mirror, reflecting the practitioner's own potential for greatness. He becomes a guiding force, not by granting fame as a gift but by revealing the pathways through which one can achieve it.

Engaging in magikal practices to attain fame under Satan's guidance often involves rituals and spells that are as much about self-empowerment as they are about external influence. These practices might include visualization techniques to clearly see oneself in a position of fame, incantations to attract the energies of recognition and influence, and perhaps even talismanic magik to carry the essence of one's ambitions into the physical world.

However, this journey is not without its ethical dilemmas. The pursuit of fame, especially through magik, raises questions about personal integrity, the impact on others, and the true cost of fame. Working with Satan in this context demands a deep introspection about one's motives, the readiness to face the responsibilities that come with fame, and the wisdom to use such power judiciously.

Seeking fame and celebrity status through magikal practices with the aid of Satan is an exploration of ambition, power, and the desire for recognition. It is a path that requires not only magikal prowess but also a deep understanding of one's own desires, the courage to chase them, and the wisdom to handle the fame that might follow. This chapter aims to guide the reader through this complex and intriguing landscape, offering insights into how to approach this unique and powerful path in the world of magik.

HISTORICAL AND CULTURAL CONTEXT OF FAME IN MAGIK

In the enigmatic corridors of history, the intertwining of fame, celebrity, and occult practices casts a long, intriguing shadow. This section peels back the layers of time to explore how the quest for fame and the allure of celebrity status have been pursued through various occult traditions, and how the figure of Satan has evolved within this context.

From the mystical courts of ancient Egypt to the secretive societies of medieval Europe, the desire for fame has often been entwined with the occult. In ancient times, fame was not merely about public adoration but was also seen as a form of immortality, a way to etch one's name into the annals of history. Sorcerers, magicians, and wise men were often believed to wield the power to grant fame and fortune to those who sought it, using rituals and spells that were as much an art as they were a science. These practices were shrouded in secrecy, accessible only to the initiated, and were often closely linked with the worship of deities and entities that personified power and influence.

Throughout history, several notable figures have been associated with using occult practices to gain fame. These range from legendary sorcerers like Merlin, who was said to wield great influence in the royal courts, to historical figures like John Dee, an advisor to Queen Elizabeth I, known for his esoteric practices and quest for knowledge. In these tales, whether myth or reality, we see a recurring theme: the use of magik not just as a means to personal power, but as a pathway to recognition and influence on a grand stage.

The figure of Satan, within the context of fame and the occult, has undergone a significant transformation over the centuries. Initially depicted as a malevolent force, Satan gradually came to be seen by many occult practitioners as a symbol of rebellion against the orthodox, a champion of personal ambition, and a guide to unlocking one's full potential. In the pursuit of fame, Satan has been invoked as a powerful ally, one who could grant not just material success but also the charisma and allure that come with celebrity status.

The cultural perception of fame and its relationship with the occult has also evolved. In ancient times, fame achieved through magikal means was often viewed with awe and respect. In contrast, during periods like the European witch trials, any association with fame and the occult could be dangerous, even deadly. In modern times, the interplay between fame, celebrity, and the occult has often been sensationalized, sometimes viewed with skepticism but always with a hint of fascination.

The historical and cultural journey of fame in occult practices reveals a fascinating landscape where ambition, power, and the supernatural meet. This exploration not only sheds light on how the desire for fame has been pursued through the ages but also helps us understand the evolving nature of magikal practices and the complex figure of Satan within this pursuit. As we turn the pages of history, we uncover a narrative that is as much about the human desire for recognition and legacy as it is about the mystical pathways that promise to lead there.

MYTHS: SELLING YOUR SOUL

In the shadowy online forums and real-life groups, focusing on fame and magik, where whispered legends and half-truths dance together in the flickering candlelight, there persists a myth as old as time - the selling of one's soul to Satan. Let's unravel this myth, exploring its origins and the truths hidden beneath its enduring facade.

Too long: Didn't read = No, you can't sell your soul. It's not like it's an extra kidney you're not currently using.

The longer version:

A DEAL WITH THE DEVIL

The story goes that one can gain fame, fortune, and earthly pleasures beyond imagination by offering their soul to Satan. It's a narrative steeped in folklore, often depicted in tales of desperate individuals meeting the devil at a crossroads, especially in the sultry twilight of the American South. The crossroads - a place where paths converge and choices must be made - becomes the stage for this age-old drama.

However, in the reality of occult practices, Satan is not in the business of trading for souls. This idea is a myth, a dramatic creation that has been perpetuated through centuries of storytelling and sensationalism. In truth, the figure of Satan in magik is more about the pursuit of knowledge, personal power, and breaking free from societal and self-imposed chains. The concept of Satan dealing in souls reduces this rich, complex archetype to a mere caricature, an entity playing a numbers game in a cosmic competition for souls.

The crossroads myth, while not literally true, holds significant symbolic weight. It represents a point of decision, a moment where one must choose which path to follow. In magik, meeting Satan at a crossroads is a metaphor for confronting one's deepest desires, fears, and ambitions. It's a ritualistic acknowledgment that the pursuit of fame and celebrity through magik is a journey fraught with choices and consequences.

In Daemonic and Satanic magik, the soul is not a currency to be bartered but a reflection of one's journey. Your soul, in this context, is the essence of who you are - your desires, your fears, your ambitions, and your moral compass. Engaging with Satan in magikal practices is about aligning this essence with your magikal intentions, not about relinquishing it.

The myth of selling one's soul to Satan for fame and fortune is just that - a myth. It's a narrative that has grown and evolved, capturing imaginations but obscuring the true nature of occult practices. In reality, the journey with Satan in the pursuit of fame is about self-discovery, empowerment, and understanding the true cost and value of what one seeks. It's a path of enlightenment, where the soul is not lost but is instead fully realized.

NAVIGATING THE SPIRITUAL AND ETHICAL IMPLICATIONS

In the pursuit of fame through Satan-centric magik, the path is strewn not just with the petals of success, but also with the thorns of spiritual and ethical dilemmas. This critical section delves deep into the labyrinthine world of fame magik, exploring the intricate balance between personal ambition and spiritual integrity, and the ripples such pursuits create in the fabric of one's personal life and relationships.

Walking the tightrope between ambition and spiritual integrity in the world of fame magik is akin to navigating a mystical forest, where each step could either lead towards enlightenment or into a thicket of ethical quandaries. On one hand, there's the burning desire for fame, recognition, and influence, fueled by the potent energies of Satan-centric magik. This path is enticing, lined with the promises of public adulation and the power that comes with influence.

However, this pursuit is not without its spiritual cost. The relentless quest for fame can often lead to a disconnection from one's inner self, a loss of spiritual grounding. It's crucial to constantly check in with your moral compass, ensuring that your quest for fame does not lead you astray from your true spiritual path. It's about using the powers granted by such magik not just for personal gain but also in ways that align with your deeper, spiritual self.

The quest for fame, especially when bolstered by magik, can have a profound impact on one's personal life and relationships. It's like casting a stone into a still pond – the ripples spread far and wide. Relationships may be strained or altered as one's priorities shift. The allure of the spotlight can sometimes overshadow the value of private, personal connections. It is essential to remain mindful of these changes, ensuring that the pursuit of fame does not lead to a life of isolation or disconnection from those who matter most.

With great power comes great responsibility – a timeless truth that holds particularly true in the realm of fame magik. The influence you gain over the public is not just a tool for personal advancement; it's a mantle of responsibility that needs to be carried with care and wisdom. How you wield this influence can have far-reaching consequences. It's about being mindful of the messages you convey and the impact you have on your audience. The ethical use of this influence is paramount, ensuring that it contributes positively to the collective consciousness rather than leading others astray.

Navigating the spiritual and ethical landscape of Satan-centric magik for fame is a journey fraught with complex choices and profound introspection. It's a magikal dance that requires a delicate balance, a constant alignment of one's spiritual and ethical values with their personal ambitions. As you turn the pages of this chapter, let it be a guide to understanding the deeper implications of fame magik, reminding you that the pursuit of fame is not just a journey outward into the spotlight but also an inward journey of spiritual and ethical discovery.

RITUAL FOR ACHIEVING FAME IN CHOSEN FIELD

Embarking on a ritual to seek the assistance of Satan in achieving fame in your chosen field is a profound undertaking. It involves a deliberate alignment of your intent, energies, and actions to manifest your aspirations into reality. The following ritual is designed to tap into the powerful energies associated with Satan for this purpose.

Write out your petition before working this ritual. On the parchment paper, write your specific aspirations using the black or gold ink pen. Pour your ambition, desire, and dedication into each word.

Items Needed:

A black altar cloth

Altar candles in all black

A representation of your chosen field (e.g., a musical instrument for a musician, a pen for a writer)

A red candle (symbolizing ambition and desire)

Incense (preferably one that aligns with power and success, like dragon's blood)

Satan's Material Mastery and Earthly Power Sigil

A piece of parchment paper

A black or gold ink pen

Offering - blood offering, diabetic lancet and fire proof bowl.

Actions:

Symbolic Representation: Place the item representing your chosen field in the center of the altar. This item serves as a physical embodiment of your career aspirations and goals.

Cast your circle, and light the altar candles. Turn off the room's lights.

Light the incense, allowing its aroma to fill the space. Incense acts as a medium, carrying your desires and intentions into the ether.

Light the red candle, allowing its flame to symbolize the burning desire within you for fame and success in your field. The candle's light is a beacon, calling forth the energies you seek to harness.

Place Satan's Sigil on the altar. Stand before it and respectfully invoke Satan by saying:

Lord Satan!

Renich uberace ninan vesa Ave Satanis

Renich uberace ninan vesa Ave Satanis

Renich uberace ninan vesa Ave Satanis

Ave Satan! I summon thee!

I ask that you join with me now

In my sacred circle.

I have a request to ask of you!

Express your desire for fame and success in your chosen field. Be clear and specific about your goals, and ask for Satan's assistance in achieving them.

Take your written petition/statement, fold the paper and hold it over the candle's flame (without burning it), symbolizing the transfer of your desires into the realm of magik.

Thank Satan for his presence and assistance. Take the diabetic lancet, poke a finger (any finger, either hand) and place a single drop of blood onto the sigil. Touch the paper to a candle flame, and allow the paper to burn fully, dropping it into the fireproof bowl.

While doing this, say: ***Lord Satan, I thank you for your presence here tonight, please accept this humble offering of my essence in gratitude for your help in this matter.***

Snuff out the candle, symbolizing the completion of the ritual and the beginning of your journey towards fame. Keep the parchment in a safe place, such as under your pillow or in a special box, as a continuous reminder of your intent.

Regular Reinforcement: Repeat this ritual at regular intervals, such as once a month, to reinforce your intent and maintain alignment with your magikal goals.

This ritual is a powerful tool in your magikal practice, designed to align your ambitions with the energies of success and recognition. Approach it with respect, clarity of intent, and an open heart, ready to receive the guidance and assistance you seek in your journey to fame.

RITUAL FOR MAGIK ASSISTANCE IN ACHIEVING CELEBRITY STATUS OR GAINING GREAT SOCIAL MEDIA INFLUENCE

In the modern age, where celebrity status and social media influence are coveted treasures, turning to magik for assistance can be a powerful tool. This ritual, designed to call upon Satan for aid in achieving these goals, intertwines the ancient with the contemporary, creating a bridge between timeless energies and modern aspirations.

The aspect we'll be calling in this ritual is the Material Mastery and Earthly Power aspect. Use this specific sigil in the ritual below.

You should prepare a petition before the ritual itself, just to work out the best wording. Remember, be specific, and cover all loopholes.

For this, you will need to be ready to work a blood offering.

Although this type of ritual can be worked at any time or day of the week, it might work better on a Sunday or Monday, due to the connection between those days and achieving fame.

Items Needed:

The Altar candles in black and red

Altar cloth

Your petition

A digital device (phone, tablet, or computer) symbolizing your connection to the digital world

A blue candle (representing communication and influence)

Frankincense or myrrh incense - stick is fine, but I prefer the resin

Satan Material Mastery and Earthly Power Sigil

A quartz crystal (for clarity and amplification of intent)

A small bowl of water (symbolizing emotional connectivity with your audience)

Diabetic lancet and spare sigil, plus fireproof bowl.

The Ritual

Arrange your altar as best suits you. Place your digital device on the altar. This device represents your gateway to social media influence and celebrity status, a tool through which your influence will flow.

Light the altar candles, room lights off, then light the blue candle. As the blue candle's flame flickers, visualize it casting a wide, illuminating glow, symbolizing the spread of your influence across the digital realm.

Drop some incense on the coal (or light the stick), letting the aromatic smoke symbolize the dissemination of your presence and essence through the ethers of the internet.

Place Satan's Sigil on your altar, signifying your call to his power and assistance in your quest for fame and influence.

Next, place the quartz crystal near your digital device and the bowl of water near the blue candle. The crystal acts as a beacon of clarity and amplification for your intentions, while the water represents your emotional connection with your audience.

Now, we invoke Satan using this specific summoning:

Lord Satan!

Renich uberace ninan vesa Ave Satanis

Renich uberace ninan vesa Ave Satanis

Renich uberace ninan vesa Ave Satanis

Ave Satan! I summon thee!

I ask that you join with me now

In my sacred circle.
I have a request to ask of you!

Articulate your desire for celebrity status or social media influence. Speak clearly of your intentions to reach a wide audience and to wield influence responsibly and effectively.

Read your petition, which will formally ask Satan for his assistance, making sure your petition covers all details.

Hold your hands over the blue candle (at a safe distance) and the digital device, imagining a link forming between the flame, the device, and your intent. Visualize your social media presence growing, your messages reaching far and wide, and your influence expanding.

To close, thank Satan for his guidance and influence. Extinguish the candle and incense, symbolizing the completion of the ritual but the beginning of your journey towards achieving your goals.

Prepare the blood offering by pricking a finger (and finger, any hand) and dropping a single drop of blood onto Satan's sigil. Touch the sigil to a candle flame, and allow it to bring completely, while saying:

Lord Satan, I thank you for your presence here tonight, please accept this humble offering of my essence in gratitude for your help in this matter.

Repeat this ritual periodically, especially during key times for social media activity or when seeking to boost your public presence.

Approach this ritual with a sense of seriousness and respect for the powers you are invoking. Remember, the path to celebrity status or social media influence is not just a journey of external growth but also one of internal development and responsibility.

CHAPTER 10

SPIRITUAL ASCENSION AND ENLIGHTENMENT - SATAN AS INITIATOR AND GUIDE

As part of my life's mission, only revealed to me later in life, I am to assist as many people as possible towards true enlightenment. The first step is to chuck out all those dogmatic tomes from various religions, and yes - not just the Brand Name Religions count; Golden Dawn, Wicca, and the rest also count as religions.

As part of this, I now turn to the magik of enlightenment, using Satan. Looking at this, and bypassing the trappings of dogma, the figure of Satan emerges not as an adversary, but as a profound initiator and guide. This section explores the unconventional yet deeply insightful role of Satan in the spiritual realm, elucidating how this misunderstood entity can be a catalyst for profound personal transformation and enlightenment.

The Unconventional Mentor: Satan's Role in Spiritual Growth

To truly grasp the intricacies of Satan's role in spiritual ascension, it is imperative to traverse beyond the conventional narratives that have long painted this figure in a singular, often malevolent light. Within the rich and complex tapestry of occult practices, Satan is venerated not as a mere symbol of evil or chaos, but as a profound embodiment of knowledge, freedom, and self-empowerment. This perspective requires a paradigm shift, a willingness to view Satan through a lens unclouded by centuries of dogma and misunderstanding.

In many esoteric traditions, Satan is perceived as the ultimate iconoclast. He is the challenger of norms, tirelessly questioning the unquestioned and tearing down the walls of traditional dogma that have confined spiritual thought for ages. His role is akin to that of a spiritual revolutionary, one who prompts critical thinking and encourages individuals to forge their own paths to enlightenment. This aspect of Satan embodies the quest for truth, urging seekers to delve into the depths of knowledge, often hidden or forbidden in mainstream religious practice.

Satan, in this context, is also a harbinger of freedom. He represents liberation from the shackles of spiritual stagnation, offering an escape from the confines of conventional spirituality that may limit personal growth and understanding. His energy is one that catalyzes change, propelling individuals towards a journey of self-discovery and liberation. In Satan's domain, freedom is not just a concept, but a lived experience - a chance to explore one's true will, free from societal and self-imposed constraints.

Furthermore, Satan, as a symbol of self-empowerment, stands at the vanguard of personal development in the spiritual realm. He encourages individuals to tap into their inner strength, to harness their will, and to actualize their potential. This path of empowerment is not one of submission to an external deity, but rather a journey of becoming one's own god, mastering one's destiny, and realizing the divine within. It is a journey that demands courage, for it involves facing the darkness within and transforming it into a source of power.

The portrayal of Satan in this enlightened role challenges practitioners to reassess their understanding of good and evil, light and dark, knowledge, and ignorance. It invites them to embrace a more holistic view of the universe, where enlightenment is found not in the rejection of the shadow, but in its understanding and integration. In this light, Satan emerges not as an adversary to spiritual ascension but as a crucial ally, guiding seekers through the labyrinth of their inner worlds to emerge enlightened, empowered, and truly free.

Initiator into Mysteries

Satan, as an initiator in the esoteric journey, stands at the forefront of the unknown, beckoning the seeker to venture beyond the veil of the mundane. In this enigmatic role, he embodies the essence of a gatekeeper, guarding the portals to profound wisdom and deeper mysteries of existence that are often shrouded from the conventional seeker. This initiation process, under Satan's guidance, is far from a simple or gentle introduction to hidden realms; it is a transformative experience, marked by intensity and profound revelations.

The role of Satan as an initiator can be likened to a masterful guide leading an expedition into uncharted territories. He challenges the seeker to question their deepest beliefs, to confront the fears and doubts that have held them back, and to embrace the uncertainty that comes with exploring the depths of spiritual knowledge. This journey with Satan is not for the faint-hearted; it demands courage, resilience, and an unwavering desire for truth. It's a path that promises to unravel the fabric of reality as one knows it, revealing layers of existence that are often invisible to the uninitiated eye.

In this initiation, Satan presents the keys to unlock secrets that lie beyond traditional spiritual paths. These keys are not literal but metaphorical, representing the tools and insights necessary to navigate and comprehend the complexities of the spiritual universe. They symbolize the unlocking of latent potential within the seeker, the activation of higher consciousness, and the acquisition of esoteric wisdom that has been kept hidden from the mainstream narratives of spirituality.

This awakening, overseen by Satan, is often characterized by a series of revelations and epiphanies that can be both exhilarating and overwhelming. The seeker is exposed to new realities and truths that may radically alter their perception of the world and their place within it. This is not merely an accumulation of knowledge but a recalibration of the entire being—mentally, emotionally, and spiritually. The initiation process is akin to a metamorphosis, where the seeker emerges transformed, armed with a deeper understanding of the cosmos and a renewed sense of purpose.

Moreover, the role of Satan as an initiator challenges the seeker to embrace the duality of light and darkness within themselves and the universe. It encourages an exploration of the shadow self, understanding that enlightenment does not come from the denial of darkness, but from its integration and acceptance. Through this intense process of initiation, Satan guides the seeker to a state of balance and wholeness, where the polarities of existence are not in conflict but in harmonious coexistence.

This is a journey that transcends the superficial layers of spiritual practice, plunging the seeker into the depths of the occult and the hidden realms of consciousness. This initiation is a profound awakening, a radical shift in understanding that forever changes the seeker's relationship with the spiritual world.

Guide to Self-Discovery

When it comes to the intricate tapestry of spiritual ascension, Satan's role extends beyond that of an external guide. In contrast to a conventional mirror that merely shows one's superficial image, this particular mirror goes beyond the surface and plunges into the profound depths of one's being, laying bare their innermost desires, fears, and the expansive realm of undiscovered potential. Engaging with Satan in a spiritual context is thus a journey of introspection and self-discovery, a venture into the uncharted territories of one's own soul.

This process of self-discovery with Satan as a guide is akin to venturing into a labyrinth. The seeker navigates the winding paths of their inner world, guided by the illuminating yet challenging light of Satan. In this journey, one encounters the shadow self – the aspects of personality and psyche that are often suppressed, neglected, or ignored. These may be traits, desires, or aspects of one's identity that have been deemed unacceptable or uncomfortable, pushed into the shadowy recesses of the subconscious.

Confronting the shadow self is an integral part of spiritual growth, but it is by no means a straightforward task. It often involves facing deep-seated fears, unresolved conflicts, and uncomfortable truths about oneself. It's a journey that requires courage, honesty, and a willingness to face one's inner demons. In this context, Satan serves not as a figure of fear or evil, but as an embodiment of truth – a catalyst urging the seeker to confront and integrate these hidden aspects of themselves.

The process of self-discovery and shadow integration is essential for true spiritual growth and self-awareness. It is through acknowledging and embracing every part of oneself – including those aspects considered dark or undesirable – that one can achieve a state of wholeness and balance. Working with Satan in this capacity is about harnessing his energies to illuminate the hidden corners of the self, bringing light to the darkness, and finding power in what was once weakness or fear.

Additionally, this process of self-exploration often results in the realization of hidden abilities in the individual. Hidden talents, strengths, and abilities that have been buried under layers of self-doubt, societal conditioning, or fear are brought to the surface. Satan, in this role, acts as an enabler, encouraging the seeker to explore and develop these newfound aspects of themselves.

In essence, Satan, as a guide to self-discovery, offers a path to profound self-knowledge and empowerment. It is a journey that not only transforms the seeker's understanding of themselves but also alters their interaction with the world. This path, while fraught with challenges and introspective trials, ultimately leads to a place of greater authenticity, power, and spiritual enlightenment.

The Light of Enlightenment in Satan's Wisdom

In the world of Satan-centric magik, the pursuit of enlightenment takes on a dimension that is markedly different from the serene, transcendent states often associated with mainstream spiritual practices. Here, enlightenment is envisioned not as a gentle, diffusing glow but as a fierce, blazing inferno that lights up the deepest, most hidden recesses of the soul and the cosmos. This form of enlightenment, represented through the wisdom of Satan, challenges conventional notions, inviting practitioners into a space where complexity, pain, and contradiction are not just acknowledged but embraced as integral parts of the journey.

This unique perspective on enlightenment acknowledges that true understanding and wisdom often come from confronting and engaging with the darker, more difficult aspects of existence. In this context, Satan emerges as an emblem of this unflinching pursuit of truth. He embodies the courage to face the abyss, to stare into the heart of darkness, and find within it the seeds of light. It is a journey that requires not just intellectual understanding but emotional and spiritual bravery.

The light of enlightenment in Satan-centric magik is akin to the alchemical process of turning lead into gold. It involves transforming the base, primal aspects of our nature into something higher and more refined. This process is fiery and intense, mirroring the often tumultuous journey of personal and spiritual growth. Through this, Satan becomes a symbol of the inner fire that burns away ignorance and illusion, revealing a more authentic and empowered self.

Moreover, this form of enlightenment does not seek to escape the realities of pain, suffering, or contradiction, but rather to understand and integrate them. It recognizes that these elements are as much a part of the human experience as joy, peace, and harmony. Satan, in this role, serves as a guide through these complexities, offering his wisdom to navigate the paradoxes and challenges that inevitably arise on the path to enlightenment.

In Satan-centric magik, enlightenment is therefore seen as a dynamic, ongoing process rather than a static, final state. It is about continually evolving, growing, and adapting, always seeking deeper levels of understanding and awareness. This path of enlightenment is richly textured, colored with the full spectrum of human experience, and Satan stands as a beacon, illuminating the way forward with his unorthodox and profound wisdom.

In essence, the light of enlightenment in Satan's wisdom is a radical departure from traditional spiritual narratives. It offers a path that is rigorous, deeply challenging, and immensely rewarding, demanding a full engagement with all aspects of life and self. Through this journey, practitioners are invited to explore the full depth and breadth of their being, emerging with a profound understanding that true enlightenment encompasses the entire spectrum of existence, from the darkest shadows to the brightest light.

The path of spiritual ascension with Satan is not one of passive acceptance, but active engagement with the deepest aspects of the self and the universe. It's a journey that promises not just spiritual elevation but a profound redefinition of what it means to be enlightened.

SATAN AS THE REAL LIGHT OF ENLIGHTENMENT

When exploring the enigmatic and esoteric realms of spiritual wisdom, the persona of Satan often conjures images of obscure shadows and unyielding rebellion. Within the expansive realms of magik and enlightenment, where the depths are explored, Satan transcends his role as a mere harbinger of doom and instead emerges as a luminous beacon, radiating the utmost profound and enlightening illumination. With that in mind, I'm going to examine into the concept of Satan as a symbol of genuine enlightenment, pushing boundaries and offering new interpretations of spiritual awakening.

The Misunderstood Luminary

The figure of Satan often bears the burden of widespread misconceptions when it comes to the subject of Enlightenment. Commonly portrayed as the quintessence of evil and darkness in mainstream narratives, his true essence in many esoteric traditions is starkly different. Far from embodying malevolence, Satan symbolizes a form of enlightenment that is raw, unfiltered, and deeply transformative – a stark contrast to traditional views of spiritual illumination.

This enlightenment is not the serene, comforting light often depicted in conventional spiritual imagery. Instead, it is a piercing, revealing flame that cuts through facades and superficiality. Satan, in this profound role, is seen as the bearer of a light that does not blind with its brilliance, but instead reveals the truth. This light is a metaphor for knowledge and awareness that brings clarity, piercing through layers of ignorance and misunderstanding. It is a light that demands courage to behold, for it illuminates the darkest recesses of the human psyche, laying bare the truths that lie hidden in shadow.

In the process of spiritual ascension, this light plays a crucial role. It encourages introspection, a deep and often uncomfortable examination of the self. Satan, as the bringer of this light, challenges individuals to confront their fears, weaknesses, and hidden desires. This process is far from easy or pleasant; it often involves facing painful truths and dismantling long-held beliefs. However, it is through this rigorous introspection and confrontation with the self that genuine growth and understanding occur.

Furthermore, Satan's form of enlightenment is one of empowerment. By illuminating the darker aspects of one's psyche, he enables individuals to understand and integrate these aspects, transforming weaknesses into strengths and fears into wisdom. This path of enlightenment is about embracing the entirety of one's being, including the parts that are often shunned or suppressed. It's about recognizing the power and potential that lies within these shadowed parts of ourselves.

In many occult traditions, therefore, Satan is revered not as a corrupter but as a liberator. He is seen as a guide who leads seekers through the darkness to find their own inner light – a light of true knowledge, freedom, and self-realization. His illumination brings a deeper, more holistic understanding of the self and the universe, transcending conventional notions of good and evil, light and dark.

In essence, the role of Satan in spiritual ascension is that of an enlightener who challenges and supports the seeker in equal measure. His light is one that brings about profound transformation and self-discovery, guiding individuals to a more authentic and empowered form of spiritual awakening. This path, marked by Satan's unique form of enlightenment, is a journey towards a deeper, more encompassing understanding of existence and one's place within it.

ENLIGHTENMENT BEYOND THE CONVENTIONAL

In the diverse landscape of spiritual journeys, the conventional image of enlightenment is often one of serene detachment, a state where the practitioner transcends worldly concerns and achieves a state of blissful peace and wisdom. This portrayal typically depicts a gentle, almost passive process of spiritual awakening, marked by a gradual detachment from the material world and a quiet, introspective journey inward. The ultimate goal in such a narrative is often to reach a state of nirvana or liberation, where the soul is free from the cycle of rebirth and suffering, basking in eternal peace.

However, when one embarks on a path of enlightenment with Satan as a guide, the experience diverges dramatically from these traditional portrayals. In this less-trodden path, enlightenment is not a quiet, gentle bloom opening to the sun but a fierce, blazing fire that consumes all falsehoods, illusions, and superficialities. This process is far from the tranquil, detached awakening often depicted; it is intense, passionate, and deeply transformative.

Satan, in this context, serves not as a soothing balm, but as a catalyst for profound and often radical change. The enlightenment he offers does not involve withdrawing from the world, but rather engaging with it more fully, deeply, and honestly. It's about confronting the often-harsh realities of existence, facing the shadows within oneself and the world, and finding truth and wisdom in these challenges.

This path of enlightenment is akin to the alchemical process of calcination, where intense heat is used to purify and transform substances. Similarly, the journey with Satan as a guide involves burning away the layers of ego, societal conditioning, and self-imposed limitations. It's a purification process, but one that is vigorous and intense.

In this intense awakening, enlightenment is found in the deep immersion into reality, rather than in escape or detachment from it. It's about understanding and embracing the full spectrum of human experience, from joy and love to pain and suffering. This form of enlightenment recognizes that true wisdom and understanding come from experiencing and accepting all aspects of life, not just the peaceful or pleasant ones.

Furthermore, this journey often leads to a more active form of enlightenment, where the individual is called to use their newfound wisdom and insight to effect a change in the world. It's an enlightenment that does not end with personal liberation, but extends to actively participating in the world, using one's insights to help others and address the suffering and injustices present in the material realm.

In essence, the path of enlightenment with Satan as a guide is a journey of transformation, engagement, and passionate awakening. It's a path that challenges traditional notions of spiritual ascension, offering a more dynamic, involved, and fiery route to understanding the mysteries of existence. This form of enlightenment is not about detaching from the world, but about understanding it so deeply and fully that one becomes a catalyst for change within it.

THE JOURNEY THROUGH SHADOW TO LIGHT

In the unique and transformative path of enlightenment guided by Satan, the journey is one marked by a deep exploration of the shadow self. This exploration is not a mere cursory glance at the surface but a courageous and profound dive into the depths of our innermost fears, hidden desires, and suppressed truths. It is about peeling back the layers of the self, layers often shrouded in darkness and mystery, to uncover the raw and unvarnished truths that lie beneath.

Satan's approach to enlightenment is radically different from traditional paths. It does not involve bypassing or transcending the darker aspects of the self. Instead, it calls for a direct confrontation with these aspects. This journey through the shadow is about facing the parts of ourselves that are often uncomfortable to acknowledge – our fears, our hidden desires, our suppressed anger, and our vulnerabilities. It's about recognizing and embracing these shadow elements, not as flaws or hindrances, but as integral components of our being.

Engaging with the shadow self is essential for authentic spiritual growth. Far from being a detour or distraction, it is a vital phase of the journey. The shadow, often perceived as a source of weakness or negativity, holds immense potential for insight and transformation. It is within the shadow that we often discover untapped strengths, resilience we didn't know we possessed, and insights that can profoundly shift our perspective.

In this role, Satan acts as a formidable yet empowering guide. He does not shield the seeker from the harsh truths of their inner world. Instead, he provides the courage and support needed to confront and engage with these truths. This process can be daunting and intense, as it often involves revisiting past traumas, confronting deeply ingrained fears, and challenging long-held beliefs about oneself and the world.

However, the transformation that occurs through this journey is profound. By facing and integrating the shadow self, the seeker emerges with a more holistic understanding of their being. This integration fosters a sense of wholeness and authenticity, as no part of the self is left unacknowledged or denied. Satan, as a guide in this process, encourages the seeker to transform their fears and weaknesses into wisdom and strength.

The journey from shadow to light, as guided by Satan, is therefore not a rejection or denial of the darker aspects of the self, but a journey of acceptance and integration. It is about finding enlightenment not despite the darkness, but within it. This path leads to a form of enlightenment that is grounded, deeply personal, and powerfully transformative, reflecting a comprehensive understanding of the human experience in all its complexity.

EMBRACING COMPLEXITY AND CONTRADICTION

In the pursuit of enlightenment through the guidance of Satan, practitioners are invited to embrace a journey that is far from simplistic or linear. This path is characterized by an acceptance and understanding of the intricate complexities and inherent contradictions of life. The light of enlightenment offered in this context is one that shines unflinchingly on all aspects of existence, recognizing that pain, complexity, and contradiction are not obstacles to spiritual growth, but rather integral components of it.

This form of enlightenment acknowledges that the human experience is a mosaic of diverse emotions, experiences, and realities. It understands that life is not merely a collection of black and white absolutes, but is replete with shades of gray. The path with Satan as a guide does not simplify these complexities; rather, it encourages an exploration and understanding of them. Pain and pleasure, joy and sorrow, strength and vulnerability – all are seen as vital pieces of the human puzzle.

Moreover, this approach to spiritual growth does not view contradiction as a sign of weakness or confusion, but as a natural and inevitable part of the human condition. Contradictions are inherent in our nature, and embracing this fact is crucial for a deeper understanding of the self and the world. For instance, one might grapple with the duality of seeking individual freedom while yearning for connection and community. Rather than forcing a choice or a resolution, Satan's enlightenment encourages individuals to explore these dualities, to live them fully, and to find personal meaning and understanding within them.

This holistic approach also implies a willingness to confront and integrate the darker aspects of the self – the fears, the angers, the desires that are often suppressed in more conventional spiritual practices. It is through this integration that a more genuine and profound enlightenment is achieved, one that does not deny or flee from any part of the self, but rather embraces the entirety of one's being.

In essence, the path of enlightenment with Satan as a guide is a journey that embraces the full spectrum of human emotion and experience. It is a path that does not seek to escape the complexities and contradictions of life, but rather to understand and integrate them. This form of spiritual growth is holistic, inclusive, and deeply transformative, offering a more authentic and comprehensive understanding of both the self and the wider world.

THE ALCHEMY OF TRANSFORMATION

The journey of spiritual enlightenment with Satan as a guide is remarkably similar to the ancient art of alchemy, where base metals were believed to be transformable into precious gold through a combination of science and mysticism. In this spiritual alchemy, the practitioner works with the raw, unrefined elements of their human experience, aiming to transmute them into a higher, more spiritually refined state. This process, while metaphorical in nature, embodies a deep and profound transformation of the self.

Engaging in this alchemical transformation with Satan involves a deep and often intense exploration of the self. It requires examining and working with aspects of one's character and life experiences that are frequently overlooked or avoided. These might include personal flaws, past mistakes, buried emotions, and unacknowledged desires. In the magikal practice with Satan, these elements are akin to the 'lead' – they are the heavier, more challenging aspects of our existence that often weigh us down.

The process of transforming these aspects is not a superficial one. It often involves confronting uncomfortable truths about ourselves, facing our fears head-on, and challenging deep-seated beliefs and patterns. This journey can be unsettling and even painful at times, as it requires letting go of long-held notions and embracing change at a fundamental level. However, Satan, as a spiritual guide in this process, provides the necessary insight, courage, and strength to navigate this transformation.

As the practitioner progresses through this alchemical process, the 'lead' of their existence begins to change. The raw material of their experiences, emotions, and characteristics is gradually refined and elevated. This transformation leads to a profound shift in self-awareness and understanding. The individual emerges from this process with a heightened sense of clarity about their purpose, a stronger connection to their inner wisdom, and an empowered sense of self.

Moreover, this alchemical journey with Satan is not just about personal transformation, but also about how this change impacts one's interaction with the world. As the individual undergoes this metamorphosis, their relationships, actions, and perspective on life are also transformed. They begin to engage with the world in a more authentic and empowered way, using their newfound wisdom and strength to make positive changes in their life and in the lives of those around them.

In essence, the alchemy of transformation in the pursuit of enlightenment with Satan is a deeply transformative process that turns the lead of human experience into the gold of spiritual wisdom and empowerment. It is a challenging but immensely rewarding journey, leading to a form of self-realization that is authentic, profound, and truly empowering.

So, you see, Satan as the real light of enlightenment offers a path that is rigorous, challenging, and deeply transformative. It's a journey that demands honesty, courage, and a willingness to confront and integrate the darkest parts of ourselves. This path leads not only to personal enlightenment, but to a profound understanding of the universe and our place within it. It's a journey that, though fraught with challenges, offers the most authentic and empowering form of spiritual awakening.

Rituals Aimed at Spiritual Growth and Enlightenment

Now it's time to put this into practice, and begin our path towards enlightenment.

Each ritual the follows is a chapter in the story of personal transformation, a carefully woven narrative that facilitates deep introspection, growth, and awakening. Some consist of pathworking, others a form of ritual using sounds and images, but not really pathworking.

Be prepared to take notes, jotting down your visions, the images Satan is using to help you on this journey. Include your emotions as well. Some of this may be triggering, as old emotions and events are brought up to the surface. It's only then that we can face our inner-most shadows.

I'll present more pathworkings in a future chapter, as these are just for enlightenment.

Pathworking Ritual of the Shadow Self

The Pathworking Ritual of the Shadow Self is an evocative journey into the deeper corridors of the mind and soul, a magikal practice that requires not only courage but also an unwavering commitment to self-discovery and transformation. This ritual, set in a darkened room where the only source of light is the flickering flame of a solitary candle, creates an atmosphere of introspection and revelation.

The Setting

Start by preparing your room or space by ensuring the room is shrouded in darkness, save for the singular candle. This candle, ideally black to symbolize the exploration of the shadow, is placed before a mirror, arranged so that its light falls directly upon your reflection. The dimly lit mirror becomes a portal, a gateway into the depths of the subconscious.

The Pathworking

1. Begin by going into your space, where there are no distractions. Dim the lights.

2. Lighting the Candle: The act of lighting the candle is intentional and deliberate. As the match strikes and the flame comes to life, it symbolizes the awakening of awareness and the illumination of the inner self.

3. Enter Satan's Reality: Begin by speaking Satan's ENN for Transformation: Ayer secori menach typan on ca Satanis.

Next, visualize a path, a path leading to a world of red, towering mountains on each side. Walk down this path, and you encounter a tall man in red robes. He gestures, and produces a mirror. Walk forward and gaze into this mirror. you gaze into your own reflection. This is not a casual look but a deep, penetrating gaze, an invitation to look beyond the physical appearance and into the soul.

4. Conversing with the Shadow Self: In this reflective state, you begin a silent dialogue with your shadow self. This conversation delves into the realms of unacknowledged

213

feelings, hidden fears, suppressed desires, and forgotten parts of the self. It is a time to listen and to understand, to confront and to accept.

5. Embracing the Shadow: As revelations surface, you acknowledge and embrace these aspects of your shadow self. This embrace is not about judgment or condemnation, but about acceptance and integration.

6. Transformation and Integration: Through this acceptance, the shadow aspects are transformed. What was once hidden becomes a known and integrated part of the self, contributing to a more holistic and authentic existence.

7. Closing the Ritual: Satan now removes the mirror from your sight, and he gestures towards the path. You turn, and easily walk out of the red reality of Satan and back to your own space. Gently extinguish the candle, symbolizing the end of the ritual. As the smoke rises, it represents the release of old patterns and the beginning of a new journey with a more integrated self.

8. Reflecting and Journaling: Post-ritual, it is beneficial for you to spend time in reflection, perhaps journaling your experiences, thoughts, and feelings. This practice helps to solidify the insights gained and plan for integrating these shadow aspects into daily life.

The Pathworking Ritual of the Shadow Self is a powerful tool in the journey of personal and spiritual growth. It allows individuals to confront and integrate parts of themselves that are often ignored or hidden. Through this ritual, you will gain a deeper understanding of yourself, leading to greater self-awareness, authenticity, and personal power. It's a ritual that unveils the hidden treasures of the psyche, turning shadows into sources of strength and wisdom.

The Chant of Transformation

The Chant of Transformation is a profound pathworking in magikal practice, harnessing the primal power of sound and intention to facilitate deep personal change. This ritual, rooted in the belief that the voice can manifest will into reality, uses the rhythm and resonance of chanting to bring about a transformation within you. The setting and components of this ritual are carefully chosen to enhance the potency of the chants, making it a powerful tool for those on the path to growth and enlightenment.

Preparation and Setting

Choosing the Setting: Ideally, this ritual is performed in a natural setting, such as within a circle of trees or beside a flowing stream. Nature's elements serve to amplify the magikal energy and connects you to the earth's grounding forces. The chosen location should feel safe, serene, and conducive to introspection and vocal expression.

Creating a Sacred Space: You can choose to demarcate a sacred space, possibly by forming a circle with stones or natural objects. This circle acts as a boundary between the everyday world and the sacred space of transformation.

The Chanting Process

Before beginning the chant, you need to enter a meditative state, focusing on your breath and centering your energy. This preparatory step is crucial for aligning mind, body, and spirit with the intent of the ritual.

The chants used are deeply personal and reflect your current needs and aspirations. They may be traditional mantras, affirmations, or self-composed phrases that resonate with the individual's journey. These could include chants for releasing negativity, healing emotional wounds, or calling in new opportunities and strengths. Simple create your own mantra chant here. As we're all separate individuals, your particular chant will not be mine. So, I really can't suggest any for this step. Trust the process, and a chant/mantra will be revealed.

As you vocalize each chant, focus on imbuing the words with their intent and emotion. The chant for release, for instance, might be charged with the pain of past experiences and the desire to let them go, while a chant for empowerment could be filled with confidence and determination.

The rhythm of the chant is as important as the words. A steady, rhythmic chanting helps to create a trance-like state, enhancing the ritual's effectiveness. The resonance of the voice, coupled with the natural acoustics of the setting, creates sound waves that ripple through the air and your body, enacting energetic change.

The ritual gradually builds in intensity, with the chants becoming more powerful and assertive. At its peak, you may feel an emotional release or a profound sense of transformation. This moment is key to the ritual's effectiveness.

Integration and Closing

Grounding Post-Ritual: After the chanting concludes, it's essential to spend a few moments in silence, grounding the energy and allowing the transformation to settle within. You might visualize the changes taking root in your life, imagining the chant's vibrations continuing to work even after the ritual ends.

Closing the Sacred Space: Now, give thanks to the natural elements and any higher powers they invoked, acknowledging their support in the ritual. They then symbolically close the sacred space, perhaps by retracing the circle or collecting the stones.

Reflection and Continuation

Post-ritual reflection is encouraged. I encourage you to journal about your experiences, noting any insights or shifts in perception. Continuing to use the chants in daily life can help to maintain and strengthen the transformation initiated during the ritual.

Understand, The Chant of Transformation is a dynamic and deeply personal ritual in the practice of magik, one that leverages the power of voice and intention to bring about profound internal change. It's a practice that acknowledges the power of sound as a vehicle for transformation, providing a path to growth, healing, and personal empowerment.

The Journey of the Elements

The Journey of the Elements is a profoundly symbolic and introspective ritual in magikal practice, designed to align you with the fundamental forces of nature – earth, air, fire, and water. Each element in this ritual is not only a representation of the natural world but also a metaphor for different facets of the human experience and spiritual journey. This pathworking allows you to connect deeply with these elemental forces, drawing lessons and insights from each to aid in their personal growth and enlightenment.

Then we connect with Satan's Transformational aspect, via saying his specific ENN. In this case, it's Ayer secori menach typan on ca Satanis. You'll say this three times.

Preparation and Setting

Creating a Sacred Environment: To begin, set up a space conducive to the ritual. Ideally, this would be outdoors, in a natural setting where the elements are present in their pure form. However, it can also be adapted to an indoor environment, using items to represent each element. Especially in winter. Where I live now, it gets to well below freezing most winter days, so I work this inside.

Gathering Representations of the Elements: You should collect items symbolizing each element – soil or a stone for earth, incense for air, a candle for fire, and a bowl of water. These items are placed in the four cardinal directions, forming a circle, which represents the universe in balance.

Stand a moment, relax, and say: **"Ayer secori menach typan on ca Satanis, Ayer secori menach typan on ca Satanis, Ayer secori menach typan on ca Satanis"**

The Ritual Walk

Connecting with Earth: Start by standing barefoot on the earth, feeling its solidity and stability under their feet (again, not possible when there's half a meter of snow on the ground). This connection symbolizes grounding and a strong foundation, essential for any spiritual journey. It's a moment to reflect on stability, resilience, and the nurturing aspects of life. (In my area of the world, it's too cold for this step after October, until late April, so I suggest barefoot on your floor if it's laying directly on the ground. Cement is an earth element, so it'll work fine.)

Embracing Air: Moving to the incense, allow the incense smoke waft around you, symbolizing the intellect and clarity of air. This part of the journey is about embracing knowledge, wisdom, and the power of communication. It's a time to contemplate mental clarity, new ideas, and the freedom of thought.

Feeling the Fire: Approaching the candle, pass a hand safely over the flame, feeling its warmth. The fire represents passion, transformation, and the drive for change. This element teaches about the power of ambition, courage, and the transmutation of desires into action.

Immersing in Water: Finally, touch or immerse your hands in the water. This element signifies emotional depth, intuition, and adaptability. It's a time to reflect on emotional intelligence, the flow of feelings, and the ability to adapt to life's changes.

Integration and Reflection

1. Meditating on the Lessons: At each elemental station, you will meditate on the lessons that element imparts. They contemplate how these qualities manifest in their life and how they can be balanced and integrated for personal growth and spiritual enlightenment.

2. Completing the Circle: After moving through all the elements, stand in the center of the circle, symbolizing the

integration of all elements within themselves. It's a moment of unity and balance, acknowledging that each element is a part of the whole, contributing to the practitioner's journey.

Closing the Ritual

Gratitude and Release: Expresses gratitude to each element for its lessons and energies. Then symbolically release the elements, perhaps by extinguishing the candle, covering the bowl of water, and so on.

Grounding and Centering: After completing the ritual, it's important to ground oneself, perhaps by eating or drinking something, to return fully to the physical world.

Reflection and Application

Post-ritual, I again encourage you to reflect on the insights gained during the ritual. Journaling these thoughts can be helpful. You may also consider ways to incorporate the lessons and balance of the elements into their daily life, using them as guiding principles on their spiritual path.

The Journey of the Elements is a powerful ritual in the practice of magik, providing a deep connection to the elemental forces and offering profound insights into the self and the universe. It's a pathworking that fosters balance, growth, and holistic enlightenment, aligning the practitioner with the fundamental energies of existence.

THE PACT OF EMPOWERMENT

The Pact of Empowerment is a significant and transformative pathworking within the practice of magik, where you can form a symbolic agreement with Satan to foster your spiritual growth and personal empowerment. This ritual is a profound acknowledgment of one's commitment to the path of enlightenment, signifying a willingness to embrace change, confront challenges, and evolve both spiritually and personally.

Preparation for the Pact

1. Before engaging in the Pact of Empowerment, spend time in contemplation, identifying their goals and what they seek from the pact. This process involves deep introspection about one's spiritual path, personal challenges, and areas of life where growth and change are desired.

2. The ritual is performed in a space that feels safe and sacred to you. This could be an altar or any place where you feel a strong connection to the spiritual realm. The space is often prepared with items that represent the commitment being made, such as candles, stones, or symbols that resonate with your intentions.

Forming the Pact

1. The ritual begins with an invocation of Satan, calling upon his energy and presence. This invocation is respectful and acknowledges Satan as a guide and mentor. You clearly state your intentions for the pact, expressing their desire for guidance, strength, and wisdom on their spiritual journey.

Use any of the previous rituals as a guide for this pact ritual. Cast a circle, summon Satan, using his ENN *Ayer secori menach typan on ca Satanis*

2. Now, you outline the specifics of the pact. This can be done verbally, written in a book of shadows, or mentally. The pact includes specific commitments that you intend to keep,

such as engaging in regular self-reflection, actively working to overcome personal obstacles, and using your abilities and insights for positive change. The pact is deeply personal and reflects your unique path.

3. To solidify the pact, you might perform symbolic actions, such as lighting a candle, signing a written document, or anointing it with oil. These gestures are an external manifestation of the internal commitment being made.

The Exchange of Energy

In the Pact of Empowerment, there is a sense of mutual exchange. You commit to your path of growth and change, while in return, you seek the guidance and energy of Satan. This exchange is not seen as a transaction but as a mutual agreement based on respect and the shared goal of enlightenment.

Concluding the Ritual

Upon completing the pact, expresses your gratitude to Satan for his guidance and support. This gratitude is an acknowledgment of the mutual respect inherent in the pact.

The ritual concludes with closing the sacred space, perhaps by extinguishing candles or clearing the area, signifying the end of the formal ritual but the beginning of the commitment they have made.

Integration and Reflection

Following the Pact of Empowerment, you will reflect on the experience and begin to integrate the commitments made into their daily life. This may involve setting up regular practices, journaling progress, and being mindful of the opportunities to apply the wisdom and strength gained from the pact.

The Pact of Empowerment is a powerful pathworking in the practice of magik, symbolizing a profound commitment to personal growth and spiritual ascension. It represents a willing partnership with Satan as a source of empowerment, guiding the practitioner towards a more enlightened and empowered state of being.

As you engage in these rituals, you will weave your own unique stories of transformation and awakening. You learn that enlightenment is not a destination but a continuous process of growth, learning, and adaptation. With each ritual, you will draw closer to a state of wholeness and understanding, guided by the enigmatic yet empowering energy of Satan.

CHAPTER 11

Baneful Magik and Curses - Basic Baneful Magik Uses

Baneful practices, often veiled in controversy and mystery, hold a prominent place in the realm of magik. The practices mentioned, which encompass curses and hexes, are not only powerful tools, but also carry a substantial burden of responsibility. The following section will explore the various ways baneful magic can be employed, emphasizing the importance of careful contemplation when dealing with its potent forces.

Understanding Baneful Magik

Baneful magik, at its core, is about directing negative energy or intentions towards a person, situation, or object. It's the opposite of healing or protective magik and is used to bind, restrict, or harm. While often perceived negatively, baneful magik can have legitimate uses, such as stopping someone from causing harm or protecting oneself from negative influences.

The Role of Intent

The key to baneful magik is intent. This type of magik is not about spontaneous or reckless harm but a deliberate and considered decision to use magik for a specific purpose. It requires clarity of intention and an understanding of the potential consequences. As with any form of magik, the ethical implications must be carefully weighed.

Basic Applications

1. Protection Against Harm: One primary use of baneful magik is for protection, particularly when someone poses a threat. This could involve casting a binding spell to prevent a person from causing harm.

2. Justice and Retribution: In situations where legal or conventional means of obtaining justice are ineffective, some practitioners turn to baneful magik as a form of cosmic retribution.

3. Stopping Negative Influences: Baneful magik can be used to sever connections with toxic individuals or situations, effectively halting negative energies or influences.

Precautions and Considerations

1. Karmic Implications: Practitioners must consider the karmic implications of baneful magik. The energies sent out can often return in unexpected ways.

2. Clarity and Precision: It's crucial to be clear and precise in the intent and execution to avoid unintended consequences.

3. Ethical Boundaries: Establishing and adhering to one's ethical boundaries is crucial. It's vital to ask whether the action is justified and necessary.

In the practice of baneful magik, invoking the energy of Satan can add a powerful dimension to the workings. Satan, in this context, is not merely a figure of malevolence but a symbol of justice, retribution, and the darker aspects of natural law. In the next section, we will explore how curses can be crafted using the energy of Satan, ensuring they are effective, targeted, and ethically sound.

As we delve deeper into the world of curses and their association with Satan, we will unravel the complexities and responsibilities that come with this powerful aspect of magikal practice. The journey into baneful magik is a path treaded by few, and it requires not only strength of will but also a deep understanding of the forces at play and the wisdom to use them judiciously.

THE EGREGORE ASPECT IN BANEFUL MAGIK AND CURSES

When it comes to baneful magik and curses, the egregore aspect of Satan becomes particularly significant. Practitioners who tap into this aspect are not just invoking a mythic figure, but rather channeling a potent psychic force that has been fueled by centuries of human thought and emotion.

In rituals of baneful magik, invoking the egregore of Satan involves aligning oneself with this vast reservoir of energy. The practitioner, through ritual and will, connects to the egregore, drawing upon its immense power to fuel their magikal workings.

When casting curses, the egregore can be directed towards a specific target or situation. The practitioner might visualize the egregore as a dark wave or a shadowy figure, channeling the collective force with intent and precision. The curse, empowered by the egregore, is believed to carry with it the weight of the collective energies that have defined Satan throughout history.

Engaging with an egregore, especially one as charged as Satan's, requires not just skill but a deep understanding of ethical magik. Practitioners must be aware of their intentions and the potential impact of tapping into such a powerful collective force.

What makes the egregore of Satan particularly dynamic is its ever-evolving nature. As humanity's perceptions and beliefs about Satan continue to change, so too does the egregore. It's a symbiotic relationship; the egregore influences human thought and magik, even as it is shaped by them.

The egregore aspect of Satan represents a profound and potent force in the practice of baneful magik and curses. It encapsulates the collective psychic energy accumulated over centuries, offering practitioners a powerful tool for their magikal workings. However, engaging with such a force requires responsibility, understanding, and respect for its power and origins. By acknowledging and harnessing the egregore of Satan, practitioners connect to a deep and ancient current within the collective human psyche, wielding a power that is both immense and enigmatic.

Curses Using Satan

In baneful magik, invoking Satan for the casting of curses is a practice imbued with deep power and profound responsibility. This section examines into the intricate process of crafting curses with the assistance of Satan, underscoring the importance of intention, precision, and ethical consideration.

The Nature of Curses with Satan

Cursing using Satan-centric magik is not an act of petty revenge or spite. Instead, it is viewed as a serious magikal undertaking, often reserved for situations where justice, balance, or protection is sorely needed. When invoking Satan in such rituals, practitioners are tapping into a potent source of energy that embodies not just retribution, but also deeper cosmic justice.

Preparation and Intent

1. Setting the Intent: Before any curse is cast, the practitioner must be clear about their intent. This clarity is

crucial as it defines the curse's direction and impact. Intentions rooted in blind anger or unexamined emotions can lead to unintended consequences.

2. Understanding the Consequences: Curses are powerful and can have lasting effects on both the target and the caster. Practitioners must consider the potential consequences, ensuring that their actions align with their moral and ethical compass.

Crafting the Curse

1. Selecting the Appropriate Symbols: When preparing the curse, symbols and items that correspond with the desired outcome are chosen. For instance, if the curse is meant for binding, ropes or chains might be used; for a curse of banishment, images or items representing the person or situation might be selected.

2. The Invocation: The practitioner then invokes Satan, not as a diabolical figure, but as a powerful ally in the magikal working. This invocation is respectful, acknowledging Satan's power and asking for his assistance in the matter at hand.

3. Charging the Curse: The curse is charged with the practitioner's energy and intent. This might involve chanting, visualization, or other ritual actions that focus and amplify the practitioner's will and desire for justice or protection.

4. Deployment: The deployment of the curse can vary. It might involve burying the cursed item, burning it, casting it into a body of water, or simply leaving it at a crossroads.

Ethical Considerations

1. Responsibility: Practitioners must always remember that with great power comes great responsibility. Cursing should never be taken lightly and should always be considered as a last resort.

2. Reversibility: Consideration should be given to the reversibility of the curse. It is wise to craft curses that can be undone if circumstances change or if the desired outcome is achieved.

Transitioning to Breaking Curses

While the power to curse is significant, so too is the knowledge of how to break them. In the next section, we will explore the often-overlooked aspect of baneful magik – the breaking of curses. This part of the practice is vital, as it not only offers relief and protection to those afflicted by curses but also serves as a reminder of the impermanent and changeable nature of magikal workings.

Understanding both the creation and dissolution of curses provides a balanced perspective in the practice of baneful magik. It reinforces the concept that magik is a dynamic and evolving practice, one that requires continuous learning, adaptation, and ethical consideration.

Breaking Curses and Misconceptions

In the complex world of magik, the breaking of curses is an art as nuanced and intricate as the casting of them. This section looks into the methods and reasons for breaking curses, including the intriguing possibility that what is perceived as a curse may not be one at all. Each step in this process is a journey of discovery, insight, and often, liberation.

Understanding Curses

To break a curse, one must first understand its nature. Curses are like vines that entangle their victims in unseen ways. They might manifest as a string of bad luck, unexplained ailments, or a general sense of malaise. However, it's crucial to discern whether these misfortunes are truly the result of a curse or simply the ebb and flow of life's natural challenges.

The Power of Perception

The mind is a power thing. I have lost count of the people I've seen online who believe they're cursed. These folks are also perfect prey for the con artists that the world of magik has to deal with. Seriously, what is believed to be a curse is a creation of the mind. Like a shadow cast on a wall that seems like a monster, the mind can give form and power to fears and negative thoughts, creating a 'curse' where none exists. This psychological aspect of curses is significant and addressing it can be as powerful as any ritualistic breaking of an actual curse.

Often, the very act of "breaking" a curse will correct this mindset, allowing one to be free of the prison that is their own mind.

Rituals of Unbinding

A common method for breaking curses is a ritual cleansing bath. This bath usually contains specific herbs like hyssop, rue, or salt, known for their purifying properties. The practitioner immerses themselves in the water, visualizing the curse dissolving and washing away.

Another method involves casting a protective circle, calling upon protective spirits or deities, and explicitly stating the intent to break the curse. This practice is akin to erecting a shield against the negative energies of the curse.

These work fine as a passive way of dealing with targeting negative energy.

The Power of Amulets and Talismans

Wearing or creating amulets and talismans charged with protective energy can serve as a powerful counter to curses. These objects act as guardians, absorbing or deflecting the negative energy of the curse.

The Reversal Ritual

For more potent curses, a reversal ritual might be necessary. This involves taking an object that represents the curse and ritually destroying it, thus symbolically breaking the curse's power. This act might be accompanied by chants or incantations that affirm the practitioner's freedom and strength.

Psychological Unbinding

In cases where the curse is more psychological, methods such as meditation, affirmation, and even seeking professional counseling can be effective. The process involves reinforcing one's mental fortitude and dispelling the shadows cast by fear and negative thinking.

The Importance of Energy Cleansing

Post-ritual, it's crucial to cleanse one's energy field. This can be done through smudging with incense such as frankincense, grounding exercises, or spending time in nature. Cleansing ensures that any residual negative energy from the curse is dispelled.

A New Perspective

Sometimes, the journey of breaking a curse leads to an unexpected realization - the curse was a catalyst for growth and self-discovery. In these instances, what was perceived as a malevolent force becomes a challenging but ultimately beneficial influence.

Breaking curses in magik is a multifaceted process, blending ritualistic practices with psychological insights. It's a journey that requires discernment, understanding, and often, a change in perspective. Whether the curse is real or a product of the mind, the process of breaking it can lead to profound personal growth and empowerment. As practitioners navigate this process, they learn valuable lessons about the power of perception, the strength of their will, and the importance of maintaining a balanced and healthy energy field.

RITUALS FOR BASIC CURSES

This is a template ritual, meaning you can adjust it for the most baneful magik you might need. You'll be using the Egregore aspect, a most powerful ally in the world of attack and defensive magik. This also means blood offerings and being very careful how you word the petition.

When targeting anyone, get a photo and write their name on the back. Even better, obtain a sample of their essence, such as fingernails, hair, or a piece of worn clothing.

I worked a powerful bit of magik a few years ago, using the target's used sock. It doesn't take a lot, so cut the cloth into pieces. (I'll cover curse jars here as well).

As I have previously cautioned, make sure of your target. Take your time to consider any alternatives and perhaps pursue those until they stop working. Satan's shielding magik is very powerful (as well see in a bit) and can work to immediately stop any targeting negative energy.

In 2019, my daughter was riding in the back of an SUV, the driver ran a red light, causing a horrible crash. My daughter was lucky to be alive. That evening, I contacted Lilith, who then suggested a curse on the driver and that Satan would be best used. So, I went into ritual, quite angry. I used that anger to project magik at the target, and with Satan's help, this man was finally arrested for the wreck and had to serve time.

I can't say that you will see such results, but if (as in this case) the target most definitely deserves it, then baneful magik will be delivered.

This is a ritual template - designed to be changed and modified to fit the specific circumstances. I'll note what to do with any item used to tie the magik to the target and be prepared to give over a blood sacrifice. Note that I include oil and black salt. Black salt isn't the cooking black salt, but a mix of table salt and powdered charcoal. Anoint the red candle and sprinkle the salt on it to help prevent blow-back or a rebounding of the curse energy. I suggest an oil called "Black Art" oil, available online. (I have a recipe, and many of the ingredients are hard to locate, so try to buy it)

Your petition must be specific, ask Satan to deal with the target person, using forceful magik to bring them to justice, or to restrict their ability to bring harm to you (or the person you are working on behalf of), or ask Satan to exact revenge upon them. So, go into detail here. Use your imagination when crafting the petition.

Items Needed:

Altar candles - all black

Ritual candle, in red

Black Art oil

Black salt

Egregore aspect Sigil

Diabetic Lancet and fireproof bowl

If available, the target's photo and name or object tied to them

Actions:

Arrange your altar with Satan's sigil in the center. The target's items next to it, and the ritual candle to the other side.

Prepare the ritual candle by coating it in a light oil, then sprinkling the black salt all over it. Sit this in a thick candle holder.

Light the candles, light the incense, turn off the room lights.

Cast a circle, using the Lesser Banishing for this or the traditional daemonic circle casting.

Once this is done, take a deep breath, then summon Satan by saying:

Tasa reme laris Satan, Ave Satanis!

Tasa reme laris Satan, Ave Satanis!

Tasa reme laris Satan, Ave Satanis!

Lord of Darkness, I summon thee, Satan!

I ask that you be with me in my space,

I ask that you bring the full might of your demonic force upon

Pause a moment, visualize the target getting what they deserve. Pick up the photo or other item, then say your petition out loud.

Now meditate again, seeing the target being hit by the magik. Go into detail.

Light the ritual red candle. Say:

Lord Satan! Energize this candle to curse this person, (name), and bring out (what you wish to have happen).

Now, prepare the blood offering by pricking a finger (either hand and ANY finger). Drop a single drop of your blood onto the egregore sigil. Touch a corner to the candle flame. Allow sigil to fully burn out. Say: *Lord Satan, I thank you for your presence here tonight, please accept this humble offering of my essence in gratitude for your help in this matter.*

Once this is done, wrap the target's items in the petition by folding it up over the item. Take the item outside and bury it some place safe. A crossroads is traditional, but unless you live in the country, it'll be hard to find an unpaved crossroads, plus the cops take a dim view of people digging up paved crossroads. So, find a secluded area, and work quickly.

Remember that this template is meant to serve as a starting point and should be adapted to fit various scenarios. It is important to exercise caution when dealing with this type of magic.

CURSE JARS

Perhaps the simplest magik you can work, and rightfully belongs in the category "Swamp Magik". Sources for this type of magik are everywhere, and this section will look at the best one I have used, and by binding it with Satan's magik, you have a very powerful tool to deal with people who deserve this treatment.

A traditional curse jar, often referred to as a witch's jar or a spell jar, is a container used in magik to cast a curse or hex on a person or to deflect negative energies away from the creator. This container, typically a glass jar, is filled with various items believed to have magikal properties conducive to the intended curse or protection.

Crafting a Traditional Curse Jar

The process of creating a curse jar involves placing objects inside the jar that symbolize the nature of the curse or the protection you seek. Common items include sharp objects like nails or pins to cause discomfort, herbs associated with baneful magik like nightshade or blackthorn, and personal items or symbols representing the target of the curse. The jar is then sealed, often with candle wax, to trap the curse within.

When incorporating the aspect of Satan the Egregore into the creation of a curse jar, you harness an additional layer of energy aligned with the collective consciousness and the powerful, darker aspects of magik. This incorporation amplifies the jar's effectiveness, tapping into the broader energies associated with Satanic magik.

Items Needed for a Satan the Egregore Curse Jar:

1. Glass Jar: To contain and focus the curse's energy.

2. Sharp Objects (Nails, Pins, Glass Shards): To cause metaphysical discomfort or pain.

3. Herbs (Nightshade, Blackthorn, Wormwood): For their association with dark magik and protection.

4. Personal Item or Symbol of the Target: To direct the curse effectively.

5. Black Candle Wax: To seal the jar, trapping the curse energy inside.

6. Satanic Sigils or Symbols: To connect the curse jar to the energy of Satan the Egregore.

7. Paper and Ink: To write the intention or curse, imbuing the jar with a specific purpose.

Once you've made the jar, go into your space. Cast a simple circle and summon Satan with his Egregore enn: Tasa reme laris Satan, Ave Satanis!

Light the black candle. Say his ENN three times, then ask Satan to energize the jar. All while, drop the black wax on the lip of the lid, sealing the jar.

Sit the jar on the altar, attach the black candle to the top. Do this by dripping wax onto the jar's lid, and sticking the candle down. Allow the candle to burn out completely.

Once done, it's traditional to bury the jar next to the target's house. This may not be practicable, since the target may live a great distance away. Also, stalking around someone's house in the middle of the night isn't advised in this modern world, so go to a secluded area, after dark, and bury the jar deep where it'll not be discovered.

In creating a curse jar with the aspect of Satan the Egregore, you are combining traditional curse jar techniques with the potent energies of Satanic magik. This fusion intensifies the curse, harnessing the collective strength and darker energies associated with this aspect of Satan. It is crucial to approach this practice with clear intent and an understanding of the powerful forces at play. The creation of a curse jar, especially when linked to Satanic energies, is a serious magikal undertaking, reflecting the depth and complexity of baneful magik practices.

BREAKING A CURSE RITUAL

This is for when you have determined the person is indeed actually cursed. Although Satan isn't the absolute best at this, his energy can work wonders. It's like a daemon I've previously used, Marbas. It's not enough to just break the curse, we'll add removing that person's ability to work magik, especially if the source of the curse worked the magik themselves.

Thus, this working is designed to remove that power, or if from a hired magician, it simply deflects the baneful magik.

Breaking a curse is a serious undertaking in magikal practice, especially when involving the energies of Satan. This ritual taps into the transformative and protective aspects of Satanic energy to nullify the curse and restore balance.

Your petition should be written in a way that matches this sample, adjusting it for your specific circumstances.

"Lord Satan! I call upon you at this time to help me in breaking a curse. A curse that injuring (me, or other person). I ask that you act to remove this curse, breaking its bonds, and limiting or disempowering the person who sent this to me/them. Rid them of their ability to work magik in any form. Hid this from them, so that they will not know their evil work is destroyed."

Items Needed:

Altar Candles: All white for this ritual

Black Candle: Symbolizing absorption and protection against negative energies.

Salt: For purification and creating a protective barrier.

Chalice of Water: Representing emotional clarity and cleansing.

Satan's Benevolent Protector & Healing Sigil.

Piece of Paper and Pen: To write down the specifics of the curse you wish to break.

Incense (Preferably Frankincense or Myrrh): For cleansing the space and carrying prayers or intentions.

Mirror: To reflect and return the negative energy of the curse.

A simple offering of cream or honey in a small bowl.

Actions:

Light altar candles, and switch off the lights.

Cleanse your space by burning incense, allowing the smoke to fill the room.

Cast a circle, then lay a circle of salt around your working area to create a protective barrier against any external negative energies.

Light the Black Candle: As you light the candle, focus on its flame, being a source of protection and absorption of the curse's negative energy.

Set your petition face up on the mirror. This action symbolizes the reflection and reversal of the curse's energy.

Call upon Satan by saying his ENN and the summoning as follows:

> *Ayer Ganen Tepar Va Satanis!*
>
> *Ayer Ganen Tepar Va Satanis!*
>
> *Ayer Ganen Tepar Va Satanis!*
>
> *Satan, I invoke your transformative power.*
>
> *Aid me in breaking this curse, reflect its harm, and restore balance.*

Now, pick up the petition, and read it out loud.

Visualize the curse breaking: Focus on the curse's energy being absorbed by the black candle and reflected by the mirror. Visualize the curse's power diminishing and dissolving. Visualize the person who sent it never knowing their power is now gone.

Dispose of the petition. After the ritual, take the paper and burn it outside your protective circle. As it burns, imagine the curse's energy being completely neutralized.

Now, thank Satan by giving the offering. Pick up the bowl, and place it on his sigil, saying:

Lord Satan, in gratitude for your assistance this day, I humble offer to you this (item).

Extinguish the candle. Dispose of the salt and leftover materials outside your living area.

This curse breaking ritual harnesses the potent energies of Satan to counteract and neutralize a curse. It is a powerful ritual that requires focus, clarity of intent, and respect for the forces involved. As with all magikal practices, approach this ritual with seriousness and an understanding of the energies you are working with.

Chapter 12

Pacts

One of the most utilized types of magik using Satan is the making of a pact.

In the practice of magik utilizing Satan, the creation of a pact stands as a particularly significant and potent form of engagement. A pact with Satan is not a fleeting arrangement; it is a commitment that spans years, often stretching across the breadth of a lifetime. The nature of these pacts are diverse, covering a wide range of magikal practices, but they are particularly effective for goals like fame, power, political and educational achievements, and creative endeavors such as writing and book promotion.

Understanding the Nature of Pacts

1. Long-Term Commitment: A pact with Satan is akin to a long-term strategic plan for one's aspirations and dreams. It

requires foresight, planning, and a clear vision of the end goals. This is not a path for those seeking instant results, but is rather for those who are prepared to invest time and effort in pursuit of significant life achievements.

2. Multifaceted Approach: The structure of a pact often involves multiple stages or parts. Each segment of the pact is designed to build upon the previous one, creating a step-by-step approach towards the ultimate goal. This phased structure allows for gradual progression, making large and seemingly distant objectives more attainable.

3. Crafting the Pact: Creating a pact follows a similar process to crafting any ritual in magik. It begins with defining a clear objective, determining which aspect of Satan's energy to work with, and then meticulously planning the long-term steps required to achieve the desired outcome.

Examples of Pacts

These are just examples which immediately come to mind.

Career Advancement Pact: For instance, consider a pact aimed at career advancement in a specific company. The first stage of the pact may focus on securing employment at the desired firm. Subsequent parts of the pact would then concentrate on climbing the corporate ladder, with the final aim being a top executive position, like becoming the CEO.

Software Development Pact: Another example could be a pact centered around software development. This could start with magik to inspire innovative software ideas, followed by successful coding, rigorous testing, and a successful launch.

The later stages of the pact might focus on achieving widespread recognition and success, culminating in a lucrative buyout offer from a major player in the industry.

Detailed example: Achieving Success in Writing

As a writer, I have used pacts to help me with success. For this example, a pact focused on writing can be an effective tool for aspiring authors. This type of pact encompasses various stages, from the inception of a book idea to achieving bestseller status. Let's look at how a pact can facilitate each phase of the writing and publishing journey.

Phase 1: Conceptualization and Writing

(I like to say "phase", it makes this sound less occult-centric, and more of a text book, yeah?)

Inspiration and Idea Generation: The first part of the pact could focus on garnering inspiration and innovative ideas for a book. This phase involves seeking the creative spark necessary to conceptualize a unique and compelling narrative. When writing, it's best to have a plan and lay it out.

Writing Process: The next step is dedicated to the actual process of writing. Here, the pact aids in maintaining focus, discipline, and productivity, enabling you to translate your ideas into a structured and engaging manuscript.

Publishing and Marketing

Securing a Publishing Deal: Once the manuscript is complete, the following part of the pact could revolve around finding the right publisher. This includes crafting compelling queries, choosing suitable agents, and attracting a reputable publishing house.

Effective Marketing Strategies: After securing a publishing deal, the pact shifts focus to marketing and promoting your book. This phase involves devising and executing a marketing plan that increases visibility, generates interest, and builds anticipation among potential readers.

Achieving Success and Recognition

Bestseller Aspirations: The final stages of the pact target the ultimate goal of achieving bestseller status. This includes strategies for widespread distribution, engaging in successful book tours, securing positive reviews, and effectively utilizing social media and other digital platforms to reach a broad audience.

Sustained Success and Future Projects: Beyond the immediate success of a single book, the pact can also encompass long-term aspirations, such as establishing a sustained writing career, producing subsequent successful works, and becoming a recognized and respected name in the literary world.

The Role of Satanic Energy in Writing Pacts

The energy harnessed through a pact with Satan in the context of writing supports the ambitious goals of the author. Satan, as a symbol of rebellion, ambition, and transformation, empowers the practitioner to challenge conventional norms, think innovatively, and persist in the face of obstacles. This energy fuels the determination and resilience needed throughout the writing, publishing, and marketing processes.

The Process and Effectiveness

Mapping the Journey: In all examples, the pact serves as a detailed map, guiding the individual through each phase of their ambition. It's a structured approach, where each step is carefully planned and executed within the framework of the pact.

Harnessing Satanic Energy: By aligning with the energies associated with Satan, these pacts gain a powerful momentum. Satan, as a symbol and entity in magik, represents transformation, rebellion against the status quo, and the pursuit of one's deepest desires. Tapping into this energy through a pact can significantly amplify the practitioner's efforts towards their goals.

Realistic Expectations and Dedication: It's crucial for practitioners to approach pacts with realistic expectations and a dedication to the process. While the pact aligns with powerful energies, it also requires commitment, patience, and continuous effort from the individual.

Understand, creating a pact with Satan in the practice of magik is a methodical and strategic process aimed at achieving significant life goals. These pacts are long-term commitments, requiring detailed planning, a phased approach, and a deep connection with the energies of Satan. Whether it's for professional success, creative projects, or personal advancement, a well-crafted pact can serve as a formidable tool in realizing one's ambitions.

WRITING THE PACT

Most pacts use the same language, and it's often written as a contract. Sometimes, it can be a simple one paragraph statement, and other times, multiple paragraphs such as my writing example earlier.

Basically, a simple pact is what you offer Satan, then what you wish to have happen using Satan's magik, then a statement telling Satan you'll be dedicated to accomplishing the goals with his help.

An example of a short pact would be this:

I, _____ in deepest respect and admiration, hereby offer Satan [what you are offering] in exchange for [what you want].

I affirm a pact with you, Satan, is my most heartfelt desire. By signing and dating below, I do dedicate myself to [what you wish to become or have happen]

Below I offer my signature:

Then place Satan's sigil or seal here.

That's it. Pretty simple, wouldn't you say?

Now for a more complex example:

General Purpose Multi-Phase Pact

Initial Phase: Setting Intentions and Goals

The first phase of this pact involves the clear setting of intentions and goals. Here, the individual identifies the overarching objective they wish to achieve. This could range from career advancement to personal development or artistic endeavors. The key in this phase is clarity and specificity; knowing precisely what you aim to achieve sets the foundation for the pact. This phase is crucial as it aligns your mental focus and energies towards your desired outcome, creating a roadmap for the magikal work to follow.

Development Phase: Skill Acquisition and Opportunity Creation

In the second phase, the focus shifts to acquiring the necessary skills and creating opportunities that align with the set goals. If the pact's aim is career advancement, this might involve learning new skills, networking, or finding mentorship. For personal development, it might mean adopting new practices or seeking transformative experiences. This phase is about laying the groundwork and taking actionable steps towards your goals. The magik of the pact works to open doors and guide you to the right places, people, and opportunities that will aid in your journey.

Manifestation Phase: Realizing Goals and Achieving Success

The third phase is where the fruits of your labor begin to materialize. This stage is about seeing the tangible results of your efforts and the magik of the pact. Whether it's receiving a job offer, completing a personal project, or achieving a milestone, this phase is marked by significant achievements towards your initial goals. The pact's energy now amplifies your successes, ensuring that your accomplishments are not only recognized but also lead to further growth and opportunities.

Final Phase: Consolidation and Future Planning

In the final phase, the pact focuses on consolidating the achievements and planning for the future. This involves reflecting on the progress made, learning from the journey, and setting new goals. The purpose of this phase is to ensure that the success achieved is sustainable and acts as a foundation for future endeavors. The magik of the pact in this stage provides a sense of clarity and direction for the future, helping you to chart a course for continued growth and achievement.

This general-purpose pact is designed to be adaptable to various goals and aspirations. Its phased approach ensures a structured and strategic path towards achieving your objectives, with each stage building upon the last. By aligning your intentions, actions, and the magik of the pact, you create a powerful synergy that propels you towards your desired future.

You can write each phase out on its own separate sheet of paper to avoid confusion.

This example is a template, which I have used with great success:

I, _____ in deepest respect and admiration, hereby call upon Satan in his (aspect) Aspect and humbly offer up to him [what you are offering] in exchange for [in detail what you want]. This pact will last (term) (months/years) and can be terminated by me in the event the pact is not delivered by Satan, thus negating any need for further offerings.

Once this pact has been fulfilled, I shall (future offering).

I affirm that a pact with you, [Name], is my most heartfelt desire. I dedicate myself to [how you wish to change or live].

By signing below, I do dedicate myself to [what you wish to become or have happen for you.]

Below I offer my signature:

Okay - now go into detail on how the pact is to be delivered. Making sure no one is harmed, you are not harmed, money is in your country's currency, etc. You know the drill.

When working any type of pact, it's important to write it out well before the Pact ritual. This is where using a nice paper and magik ink (see appendix). For using the Egregore aspect, be ready to sign the pact in actual blood, and not plain ink. This is when a dip pen comes in handy.

Take your time writing out the pact. You'll likely make many mistakes in the writing, so be prepared with a lot of paper. I'll write out the first draft on paper with a pencil, make corrections, then start my final copy. I'll often think of more to put in the pact while copying it with magik ink, so I'll have to start over.

Then, read over the pact, making sure all aspects are covered. Like money in the currency of your country. Attracting success in a field you enjoy, not in a soul-sucking corporation which will have you drinking even before you get home at night, and targeting a love interest who is emotionally, and physically, available.

Once you have the pact written up, it's time for the Pact Ritual!

PACT RITUAL

No matter how simple or complex the pact, you will use the same ritual to activate the pact.

Work the Pact ritual the same as a normal ritual.

Have your pre-written pact with you, as well as a bottle of magik ink and a pen.

Open the ritual as previously instructed.

Summon the Satan using the Aspect Summoning (consult the Appendix).

Read your pact out loud.

If possible, wait a moment for the spirit to reply.

VISUALIZE the outcome.

Sign the pact with the magik ink. If this uses Satan in his Egregore Aspect, a drop of blood will work like a signature.

Do a small offering.

At this point, end the ritual, or burn the pact, then end the ritual.

It's debated which works best. My experience shows no difference in the ultimate outcome.

During the Pact's term:

Work weekly rituals to check in on the spirit working the pact.

During which, visualize the outcome.

A small offering to the spirit.

DO NOT try to change the pact! If you've changed your mind, run a Pact Dissolution ritual.

If there is no movement on the pact, nothing even hinting at manifesting, run a ritual to make contact and use a pendulum or Tarot to see what's holding it up.

If the desire has occurred, or the pact isn't working at all, run the Pact Dissolve ritual.

PACT DISSOLVE RITUAL

Work this under the following situations: The pact has manifested and is no longer needed, or Satan isn't doing anything and you need to "Fire" him. (Hey, it's been done. You might have chosen the wrong aspect or have even set too lofty of a magik goal. It happens. And no, Satan isn't going to harm you if you do this.)

Set up as usual with the pact you wish to dissolve (or a copy) on the altar.

Open the ritual as usual and summon the aspect of Satan you used originally.

If dissolving a non-functioning pact, let Satan KNOW why it's being dissolved. It might be issues beyond anyone's control.

If the pact has manifest, give the usual offering of thanks.

Close as usual. Dispose of the offering as usual.

WEEKLY GRATITUDE RITUALS

What sets pacts apart is the need to weekly small rituals to "check in" with Satan, talk about progress and to give a small offering.

While in a pact, it's advisable to run a simple ritual once a week, to give thanks to Satan in which ever aspect you chose for a pact.

This is a simplified ritual, with minimal tools.

Depending on which aspect you chose to enter into a pact with, you will need to work a simple ritual each week.

SIMPLE GRATITUDE RITUAL

Set up your altar space. Minimal tools or props.

Summon His Darkness in which-ever aspect you used. Use the corresponding sigil for this ritual.

Make the offering. The offering will vary by ritual and spirit.

Close the ritual in the usual manner.

Again: wait overnight or 24 hrs, then dispose of the offering.

Chapter 13

Introduction to Pathworking with Satan

Now, finally, I'll look at the various ways to work with Satan using pathworking.

I do mostly pathworking, meditation rituals now. (Once I get my website back up, find out what was causing the huge server loads, I'll reintroduce my old meditation audios on higher self) These I work while in a deep meditative state. I've created an astral office, where I will project myself and communicate with gods, goddesses, spirits... And my guides.

It's quite powerful and after some practice, with dedicated work in meditation, most anyone can do this as well. It starts with regular rituals to help familiarize yourself with the energy of the spirits you most often use, and they become familiar with you as well. Then, it sure beats all the tedious set-up and candles, incense, chanting.

Thing is, I always advise trying to run physical rituals until you can know the spirit, and know what their energy feels like. Then, when working mentally, you will be protected from outside interference and know when you actually encounter the spirit you wish to connect with.

With magik, the art of pathworking is an immensely powerful technique, offering individuals a path toward transformative growth and enlightenment. When this practice intertwines with the spirit of Satan, it unlocks profound depths of understanding, strength, and liberation. As we embark on our journey of pathworking with Satan, we delve into various aspects of his essence, each offering unique perspectives and opportunities for personal development.

You might have read other books about pathworking, perhaps even books which guide you to pathworking Satan, so I have strived to channel unique pathworkings to Satan. I have channeled the visuals that Satan himself sent me for this chapter. I'll go into some detail on the pathworkings, and in each, I also advise if you need to work any circles first. For the most part, make sure to use the correct pathworking and sigil for the aspect you wish to contact, and you'll be fine. Satan has promised me he'll behave. It's one of the base tenants of me doing this book for him.

But first.

The Essence of Pathworking

Pathworking transcends the boundaries of mere ritualistic practice, evolving into a profound and immersive exploration of the inner self and the deeper recesses of the psyche. It's an odyssey that weaves through the corridors of consciousness, tapping into realms of archetypal energies and symbolic power. When one embarks on the pathworking with Satan, they engage not merely with a figure from myth but with a powerful emblem that echoes the complexities and contradictions of the human experience and the intricate fabric of the cosmos.

At its core, pathworking is a multidimensional journey. It is a process that blends the imaginative with the spiritual, creating a bridge between the conscious and the subconscious mind. This journey is often guided by visualizations, where the practitioner traverses through vivid, symbolic landscapes, each representing different aspects of their psyche and the universal energies embodied by Satan.

The images we'll be using will be placing you into the vibrational space of Satan, allowing open communication with each unique aspect of Satan.

These are intricate mental journeys, carefully structured to lead the practitioner through a series of symbolic scenarios. Each scenario in the visualization is imbued with deep meaning, tailored to evoke emotional responses, insights, and revelations pertinent to the practitioner's spiritual growth.

Essential to pathworking is the attainment of a deep meditative state. This state allows for a heightened sense of awareness and receptivity. It's in this trance-like state that the practitioner can fully immerse themselves in the experience, allowing the conscious mind to recede and the subconscious to become more accessible and influential.

Pathworking with Satan involves an intimate interaction with the archetypal energies he represents. Satan, as an archetype, encompasses various facets – from the bearer of light and wisdom to the symbol of rebellion and transformation. Engaging with these energies allows the practitioner to explore and integrate these aspects within themselves.

In these pathworkings, Satan is more than a mythological figure; he is a symbol that encapsulates a range of human experiences and universal truths. Engaging with Satan in this context is to engage with a mirror reflecting the full spectrum of human nature – from our highest aspirations to our deepest fears.

Satan is a complex symbol representing the quest for knowledge, the challenge against authority, and the journey towards self-empowerment. He stands as a metaphor for the human struggle against limitations and the pursuit of greater understanding.

Through pathworking, you can explore different dimensions of Satan as a symbol. He represents not just rebellion or opposition, but a deeper quest for meaning and understanding. He is the embodiment of transformation and enlightenment, a guide through the trials of life and the harbinger of profound personal change.

THE JOURNEY WITHIN

Pathworking with Satan is ultimately a journey within. It's a voyage into the depths of one's own psyche, where each practitioner can confront their shadows, unearth hidden truths, and discover their inner light.

Confronting the Shadow

This aspect of pathworking involves facing one's own fears, insecurities, and suppressed aspects. Satan, as the guide, helps illuminate these shadowy areas, encouraging the practitioner to confront and integrate them.

We'll be unearthing hidden truths. The journey also leads to the discovery of hidden truths about oneself and the universe. These revelations can be transformative, offering new perspectives on personal challenges and life experiences.

Ultimately, pathworking with Satan aims at discovering one's inner light – the innate wisdom and strength that resides within. This realization is empowering, offering clarity and direction on the spiritual path.

Pathworking with Satan is a profound magikal practice that offers deep insights into the self and the universe. It's a journey that requires courage, openness, and a willingness to explore the unknown territories of the psyche. Through this practice, practitioners can achieve greater self-awareness, empowerment, and a deeper understanding of the intricate dance of light and shadow that defines the human experience.

Satan also represents the liberator in the realms of sexuality and personal freedom. This aspect of pathworking with Satan encourages practitioners to explore their sexuality, to break free from societal taboos, and to embrace their true selves. It's a journey of shedding repressions, exploring desires, and understanding the sacredness of sexual energy as a potent source of magikal power and self-expression.

Satan the Egregore

Next, the egregore aspect of Satan represents the collective consciousness and power generated through centuries of belief, fear, and reverence. Engaging in pathworking with this aspect connects practitioners to a vast reservoir of psychic energy. It's a journey that transcends individual experience, tapping into the collective stream of human consciousness and its dark, powerful currents.

This aspect, you will need to work a circle and use caution, making sure you have phrased your request with care.

Get ready to embark on these diverse paths of working with Satan, and as you do, it's important to approach with respect, openness, and a readiness to be transformed. Each aspect of Satan offers a unique lens through which we can explore and understand different facets of existence, from our deepest internal struggles to the broader machinations of the world around us. Pathworking with Satan is not just about seeking external power or wisdom. It is, fundamentally, a journey of profound internal change, where the practitioner emerges not only with greater knowledge and power but also with a deeper understanding of themselves and their place in the tapestry of existence.

PATHWORKING TO THE MATERIAL MASTER AND EARTHLY POWER ASPECT OF SATAN

In another facet, Satan embodies the material master and the lord of earthly power. This pathworking focuses on the manifestation of desires, the acquisition of material success, and the understanding of earthly powers. It's a journey that teaches the balance between material wealth and spiritual well-being, emphasizing that true power comes from within and is wielded wisely and ethically.

This pathworking aims to harness energies for material success and personal empowerment in the physical realm.

Preparation

1. Create a Focused Environment: Choose a quiet space where you can concentrate without interruption. Arrange your altar or space with symbols of material success and earthly power, such as coins, stones like pyrite or citrine, and earthy elements like soil or leaves.

2. Relaxation and Centering: Begin with a few minutes of deep breathing to ground yourself. Visualize rooting yourself into the earth, your energy mingling with the stabilizing energies of the ground beneath you.

Summoning

1. Candle Lighting: Light a candle, preferably in a deep, rich color like green or gold, to symbolize material wealth and abundance.

2. Summoning Invocation: When you feel ready, recite the following invocation:

"Satan, master of the material realm, I call upon your grounding and empowering energy. Guide me to harness the power of the earth and manifest abundance and success in my physical journey."

Feel free to personalize the words to suit your connection and intention.

The Pathworking

1. Visualizing the Path: Close your eyes and envision a path leading to a grand castle or fortress, symbolizing material strength and stability. This path is lined with gold and gems, representing the richness of the material world.

2. Walking the Path: As you walk this path, focus on your material goals and desires. Feel the weight and texture of the treasures beneath your feet, symbolizing the potential for material success.

3. Entering the Castle: At the end of the path, see yourself entering the castle. Inside, find a room filled with symbols of material success tailored to your aspirations - be it wealth, property, or other forms of earthly power.

4. Meeting the Material Master: In the heart of the castle, visualize a figure representing Satan in his aspect as the Material Master. This figure radiates authority, stability, and the power to manifest.

5. Receiving Guidance: Approach Satan and present your material desires and goals. Listen or feel for guidance, insights, or affirmations about how to achieve these aspirations.

6. Thanking Satan: Once you feel the interaction is complete, thank Satan for its guidance and assurance. This can be done by simply projecting a pink light from your forehead into Satan's body.

7. Leaving the Castle: Retrace your steps out of the castle, back along the gem-laden path, feeling empowered and confident in your ability to manifest your material goals.

8. Closing the Ritual: Extinguish the candle and take a moment to ground yourself, reaffirming your connection to the earth.

Reflection and Integration

After the pathworking, spend some time in reflection. Consider the guidance you received and how you can apply it to your material pursuits. Journaling these thoughts can be particularly helpful.

This pathworking is a powerful tool for aligning with the energies of material success and earthly power. Regular practice can enhance your connection to these energies, aiding in the manifestation of your material goals and aspirations.

PATHWORKING TO THE LIBERATOR IN SEXUALITY AND LIBERATION ASPECT OF SATAN

This pathworking is focused on connecting with Satan as the Liberator in the realms of sexuality and personal freedom. It aims to explore and embrace one's sexuality, break free from constraints, and celebrate personal liberation.

Preparation

1. Creating a Comfortable Space: Choose a private and comfortable area where you feel safe and undisturbed. The space can be adorned with symbols of sexuality and liberation, such as red candles, representations of the human form, or items that symbolize personal freedom and sexual empowerment.

2. Relaxation and Grounding: Begin with deep, calming breaths. As you breathe, let go of societal judgments and personal inhibitions, preparing yourself to embrace the full spectrum of your sexual identity.

Summoning

1. Lighting the Candle: Light a red candle, signifying passion, power, and sexual energy.

2. Summoning Invocation: With a clear and open mind, recite the following:

"Satan, Liberator of the bound and Guide in the realms of passion, I call upon your empowering essence. Grant me the courage to explore and embrace the depths of my sexuality, free from constraints and full of liberation."

Personalize the invocation to reflect your intentions and desires.

The Pathworking

1. Visualizing the Path: Imagine a path leading to an ancient temple, representing self-discovery and sexual liberation. This path is lined with blooming flowers and lush greenery, symbolizing growth and natural desire.

2. Entering the Temple: Visualize yourself walking the path and entering the temple. Inside, the environment is warm and welcoming, a sacred space for sexual exploration and understanding.

3. Encounter with the Liberator: In the heart of the temple, envision a figure embodying Satan as the Liberator in sexuality. This figure is confident, radiant, and non-judgmental, embodying the essence of sexual freedom and empowerment. He is perhaps in red robes or a red suit.

4. Receiving Insights: Approach and interact with this figure. Express your desires for sexual understanding, liberation, and empowerment. Listen for insights, feelings, or thoughts that emerge, guiding you toward a deeper understanding of your sexuality and how to embrace it fully.

5. Embracing Liberation: As you receive these insights, visualize any chains or bindings that represent your sexual constraints breaking and falling away. Feel a sense of liberation, acceptance, and empowerment washing over you.

6. Thanking Satan: Once the interaction feels complete, thank the figure for its guidance and affirmation. Do this by projecting pink light from your forehead to Satan's body.

7. Leaving the Temple: Walk back through the temple, carrying with you a renewed sense of sexual identity and freedom. As you leave, feel yourself more aligned with your true sexual nature.

8. Closing the Ritual: Extinguish the candle and take a moment to reflect on the experience. Ground yourself back in the present, carrying the sense of liberation with you.

Reflection and Action

Post-pathworking, take time to reflect on the experience. Consider how you can apply the insights gained to your life. This might involve exploring your sexuality more openly, communicating your desires more freely, or simply embracing your sexual identity with greater confidence and joy.

This pathworking is a celebration of sexual freedom and empowerment, an invitation to explore and embrace the most intimate aspects of yourself, guided by the empowering energy of Satan as the Liberator.

PATHWORKING TO THE EGREGORE ASPECT OF SATAN

Pathworking to the Egregore Aspect of Satan taps into the collective energy and consciousness that this figure represents. This pathworking is designed for more shadowy aspects of magik but stops short of baneful practices, focusing instead on harnessing the collective power and wisdom embodied in the egregore for personal growth and understanding. I do not recommend working any pathworking to Satan the Egregore for the purpose of baneful magik, except for breaking possible curses.

Preparation

1. Choosing a Suitable Space: Find a quiet and private area where you can focus without interruption. The space should be one where you feel secure and undisturbed.

2. Setting the Atmosphere: Create a simple altar or focal point. This can include items like a black candle, a small mirror, and any symbols or objects that you associate with the collective consciousness or darker aspects of spirituality.

3. Grounding Yourself: Start with a few deep breaths, grounding yourself and centering your mind. Visualize roots extending from your feet into the earth, anchoring you securely.

Summoning

1. Lighting the Candle: Light the black candle, acknowledging that it represents the hidden, deeper knowledge of the egregore.

2. Summoning Invocation: When ready, say the following:

"I call upon thee Satan, Tasa reme laris Satan - Ave Satanis! Guide me in understanding the deeper, hidden currents of life and magik. Allow me to tap into your vast reservoir of knowledge, but with the wisdom to use it responsibly."

Feel free to adapt the wording to better suit your personal connection.

The Pathworking

1. Visualizing the Egregore: Close your eyes and envision a vast, shadowy figure, both present and elusive, embodying the collective energy of all those who have ever contributed to the image and idea of Satan.

2. Approaching the Egregore: Imagine yourself stepping towards this figure, feeling the weight and power of centuries of belief, fear, and respect.

3. Engaging with the Egregore: Mentally express your desire to understand the more profound and hidden aspects of life and magik. Ask for guidance in navigating these areas with wisdom and caution.

4. Receiving Insights: Stay open to any feelings, thoughts, or images that come to you. These may be symbolic or intuitive insights from the collective consciousness of the egregore.

5. Heeding Warnings: Pay attention to any warnings or cautions that arise. The egregore aspect can reveal potential dangers or ethical considerations to be mindful of.

6. Giving Thanks: Regardless of the nature of your insights, thank the egregore for its guidance and the collective wisdom it imparts. In this case, use a deep red beam of light from your solar plexus are, and direct it into Satan's body.

7. Returning from the Pathworking: Gradually bring yourself back to your physical surroundings. Extinguish the candle as a sign of completing the pathworking.

Post-Pathworking Reflection

After the session, take some time to reflect on the experience. Journal any insights or symbolic messages you received. Consider how this new understanding might influence your approach to magik and daily life.

Conclusion

Pathworking with the Egregore Aspect of Satan is a journey into the collective psychic energy that this figure represents. It's an exploration of the deeper, more hidden aspects of magik and spirituality, providing unique insights while also reminding practitioners of the responsibility that comes with such knowledge. As with all magikal practices, it should be approached with respect, caution, and an ethical mindset.

APPENDIX

GLOSSARY

1. Affirmation: Positive statements used in rituals and meditations to reinforce intent and belief.

2. Altar: A dedicated space for performing rituals and magikal workings, often adorned with symbolic items.

3. Archetype: A universally understood symbol or character that represents fundamental human experiences; in this context, Satan as an archetype represents various aspects of human nature and experience.

4. Baneful Magik: A form of magik used to bind, restrict, or cause harm, often involving curses or hexes.

5. Binding Spell: A type of magikal working intended to restrict or limit someone's actions.

6. Chant of Transformation: A ritual involving the use of voice and sound to catalyze internal change.

7. Cleansing Bath: A ritual bath incorporating specific herbs or salts for purification and removal of negative energies.

8. Egregore: A collective thought-form or psychic entity created by the beliefs, emotions, and energies of a group of people.

9. Incantation: A series of words spoken or chanted during a ritual to invoke magikal effects.

10. Invocation: The act of calling upon deities, spirits, or archetypal energies during rituals.

11. Journey of the Elements: A pathworking ritual that involves a meditative walk through representations of the four classical elements (earth, air, fire, and water).

12. Liberator Aspect of Satan: An aspect of Satan focused on sexual freedom, personal liberation, and breaking societal restraints.

13. Magik: The practice of using rituals, symbols, actions, and gestures to manipulate supernatural forces or energies.

14. Material Master Aspect of Satan: An aspect of Satan that deals with material success, wealth, and earthly power.

15. Pact of Empowerment: A ritual where a practitioner makes a symbolic agreement with Satan for guidance and strength on their spiritual journey.

16. Pathworking: An advanced magikal practice involving guided visualizations and meditative journeys for personal transformation.

17. Reversal Ritual: A ritual designed to undo or reverse a curse or negative magikal working.

18. Satan: A central figure in this book, representing various aspects of human experience and spiritual practice in magik.

19. Shadow Self: The unconscious part of the personality which the conscious ego does not identify in itself, often explored in transformative pathworking.

20. Summoning: The act of calling upon spiritual entities or energies in magikal practice.

21. Transformation and Enlightenment Aspect of Satan: An aspect of Satan focused on personal growth, self-discovery, and spiritual enlightenment.

22. Visualization: The practice of forming mental images or scenarios, often used in pathworking and other magikal rituals.

COLOR CORRESPONDENCES

Colors serve as potent visual cues to focus your intent and channel energies into your spells or rituals. Here's a basic guide to some common colors and their traditional meanings within the context of magik and spell craft:

Red

Magical Properties: Passion, love, strength, courage

Best Used: Love spells, increasing personal power, courage rituals

Orange

Magical Properties: Creativity, energy, attraction, stimulation

Best Used: Creativity spells, attraction spells, energizing rituals

Yellow

Magical Properties: Wisdom, communication, clarity, happiness

Best Used: Divination, inspiration spells, learning and studying aids

Green

Magical Properties: Prosperity, fertility, healing, growth

Best Used: Money spells, fertility rituals, healing work

Blue

Magical Properties: Calm, truth, communication, psychic awareness

Best Used: Calming spells, truth spells, psychic development

Purple

Magical Properties: Power, spiritual connection, wisdom

Best Used: Spiritual enlightenment, connection to higher powers, wisdom rituals

Pink

Magical Properties: Love, friendship, emotional healing

Best Used: Love spells, friendship rituals, emotional balancing spells

Black

Magical Properties: Protection, banishment, absorbing negativity

Best Used: Protection spells, banishing rituals, uncrossing spells

White

Magical Properties: Purity, cleansing, peace, unity

Best Used: Cleansing rituals, peace spells, general-purpose magik

Brown

Magical Properties: Stability, grounding, practicality

Best Used: Grounding spells, stability rituals, practical endeavors

Gray

Magical Properties: Neutrality, balance, veiling

Best Used: Neutralizing negative influences, balance, veiling spells

Gold

Magical Properties: Wealth, success, higher spiritual understanding

Best Used: Money spells, success rituals, higher spiritual workings

Silver

Magical Properties: Intuition, emotional balance, lunar connections

Best Used: Moon rituals, intuitive development, balancing emotions

You can customize this list based on your own experiences and intuition, as you utilize colors in your magik, you may notice specific shifts in the meanings.

TOOLS AND SYMBOLS DEFINED

Here's a list of tools and symbols commonly used in rituals involving Satan (but also refer to the specific ritual in the book):

Altar: A dedicated space for performing rituals, often personalized with items significant to the practitioner and the specific ritual.

Athame: A ritual blade or dagger, symbolizing the element of air. It's used to direct energy and delineate sacred space (casting a circle).

Book of Shadows/Grimoire: A personal magikal journal used to record rituals, spells, and insights gained during magikal practices.

Bowl of Water: Represents the element of water used for cleansing, purifying, and reflecting.

Candles: Used for illumination and focus. The altar candles for Satan vary, but I personally use black and red pillar candles. Different colors are also used to represent various intentions (e.g., red for passion, black for banishment or protection). I tend to purchase a variety pack of the spell candles, also called "chime" candles. For a holder, I prefer heavy metal holders, as the color candles are often allowed to burn out, so do not leave the candle in a fragile holder.

Chalice: Represents the element of water. It's used to hold water or wine during rituals, symbolizing the flow of emotions and intuition. A wine glass can also be used.

Diabetic Lancet: For use in blood offerings to Satan, for when you use his Egregore aspect.

Incense and Censer: Incense represents the element of air and is used for purification, setting the ritual atmosphere, and carrying prayers or intentions to the divine. The censer is the bit which holds the burning charcoal puck, on which the resin is placed. Stick incense is also fine, but I prefer the better brands without all the heavy perfume.

Magik Ink: A simple mixture. Use one drop of your blood to a small amount of drawing ink, or fountain pen ink. Use a drawing dip pen to write using this magik ink.

Mirror: Used for scrying (divination) and self-reflection. In Satan-centric rituals, it may be used for introspection or communicating with hidden aspects of the self.

Pentagram/Pentacle: A five-pointed star, often enclosed in a circle, symbolizing the elements (earth, air, fire, water) and spirit. It's a protective symbol and used to invoke energies. I have several altar cloths with the Pentacle printed on it, so it serves a dual purpose.

Parchment: Some call this magik paper. It's up to you if you wish to obtain actual magik paper, use a reputable occult shop, but expect to pay a bit for it. For myself, I use a good quality paper found at office supply shops. You know, "onion bond" with fancy watermarks.

Ritual Oil: Oils infused with herbs or essences corresponding to the ritual's intent, used to anoint candles, tools, or the practitioner.

Salt: Often used for purification and protection, representing earth, and creating sacred boundaries.

Sigils of Satan: Symbolic representations of Satan or related entities, used to focus the ritual on specific aspects or energies of Satan. The ones for this book follow. When summoning Satan in his Egregore aspect, print out a smaller sigil as well, to use in the blood offering.

Stones and Crystals: Different stones are believed to hold various energies (e.g., obsidian for protection, quartz for amplification of intentions). Because we all need more crystals, yes? (Or so the crystal shops say.)

OIL RECIPES

Black Arts Oil.

>   half a dropper essential oil of patchouli
>
>   half a dropper essential oil of black pepper
>
>   a pinch of valerian root
>
>   pinch of black poodle dog hair
>
>   a pinch of black mustard seeds
>
>   a pinch of Spanish moss
>
>   a pinch of mullein
>
>   a pinch of powdered sulfur
>
>   nine whole black peppercorns

Crush peppercorns and seeds, combine in a good carrier oil, and steep 6 weeks.

Uncrossing Oil

   2 parts Myrrh

   1 part Five Finger Grass (Cinquefoil Herb)

   Mix 2 tablespoons of this mixture to 2 ounces of carrier oil. (Olive oil or grape seed oil)

   Add a pinch of salt.

OR

   2 tablespoons of Agrimony

   2 tablespoons of rue

   2 tablespoons of peppermint

   2 tablespoons of pine bark

   You can also add some low John root as well.

   Shake well before use.

CRYSTALS

   Here's a list of common crystals and their uses in magik:

Amethyst: Known for its deep purple color, Amethyst is often used for spiritual protection and purification. It can help clear the energy field of negative influences and attachments, creating a shield of spiritual light around the body.

Black Tourmaline: A powerful grounding stone, Black Tourmaline is used for protection against negative energy. It's believed to transform dense energy into a lighter vibration, making it a valuable tool for those needing to block negativity.

Citrine: This yellow to orange crystal is popular for attracting wealth, prosperity, and success. Citrine is also known to encourage generosity and to share good fortune.

Clear Quartz: Often called the "master healer," Clear Quartz amplifies energy and thought, as well as the effect of other crystals. It's used for its high vibration, clarity, memory enhancement, and is suitable for almost any purpose in magik.

Moonstone: Known for its connection to the moon and intuition, Moonstone is revered for its ability to enhance psychic abilities and to develop clairvoyance. It's also believed to bring balance and harmony.

Rose Quartz: This pink stone is all about love. Rose Quartz is used to attract love, maintain it, and nurture a deeper emotional connection. It's also helpful for healing emotional wounds and traumas.

Selenite: Named after the Greek goddess of the moon, Selene, Selenite is used for clearing and cleansing. It can clear, protect, and shield an energy field, and is often used to cleanse other crystals.

Tiger's Eye: Known for its golden to red-brown color, Tiger's Eye is used for protection and grounding. It's believed to enhance integrity, willpower, and self-confidence.

Turquoise: A stone of protection, Turquoise is believed to be a bridge between Heaven and Earth. It's known for its healing properties and is often used for purification and dispelling negative energy.

Each crystal has its unique vibrational energy, which can be incorporated into various magik practices for enhanced spiritual, emotional, and physical wellbeing.

LINKS:

My High Magik Learning Academy - and Sigil Tutorial (FREE!)

Main site: https://highmagikacademy.com/

Sigil Tutorial: https://highmagikacademy.com/courses-page/sigil-basics-and-worksheets/

My Psychic site where you can sign up for my newsletter, and purchase signed copies of my books, or even hire me to be a mentor!

Https://davepsychic.com

Dave's Facebook Page:

https://www.facebook.com/DavePsychic/

Secrets of Magick Facebook Group:

https://www.facebook.com/groups/secretsofmagick

SATAN'S ASPECTS AND THE ENNS

This list will prove useful for when you wish to quickly connect with a particular aspect and don't feel like thumbing through this book hunting among the rituals for the right summoning.

Satan, Material Mastery and Earthly Power

ENN: Renich uberace ninan vesa Ave Satanis

Uses: Material gain, charisma, luck

Satan, Sexuality and Liberation

ENN: Ave Tasa Bunis La Satan!

Uses: Love magik, sexual magik, freedom magik

Satan the Egregore

ENN: Tasa reme laris Satan, Ave Satanis!

Uses: Compelling magik, control, baneful magik, curse breaking

Satan: Balance of Light and Darkness, Transformation

ENN: Ayer secori menach typan on ca Satanis

Uses: Personal transformation, Empowerment, Enlightenment, Shadow Work.

Satan: Benevolent Protector & Healing

ENN: Ayer Ganen Tepar Va Satanis!

Uses: Healing and protection work

SIGILS

Satan Master Sigil

Satan Master

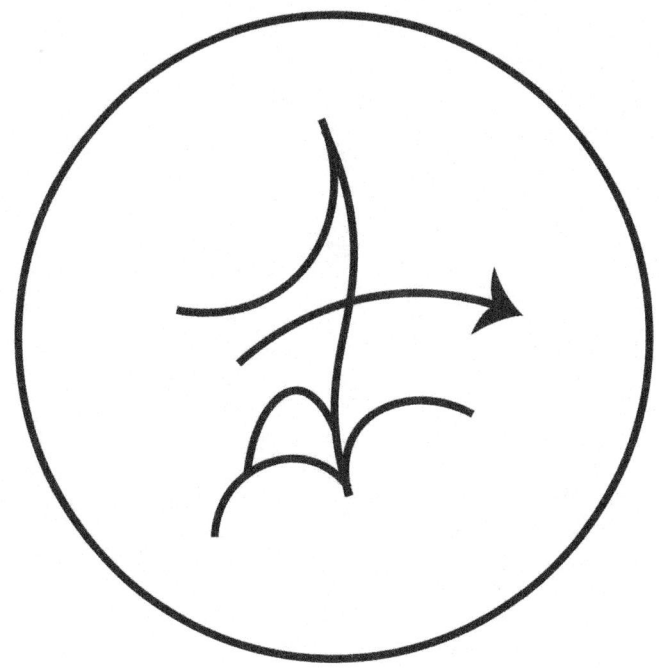

Satan's Material Masteril and Earthly Power Sigil

Material Mastery and Earthly Power

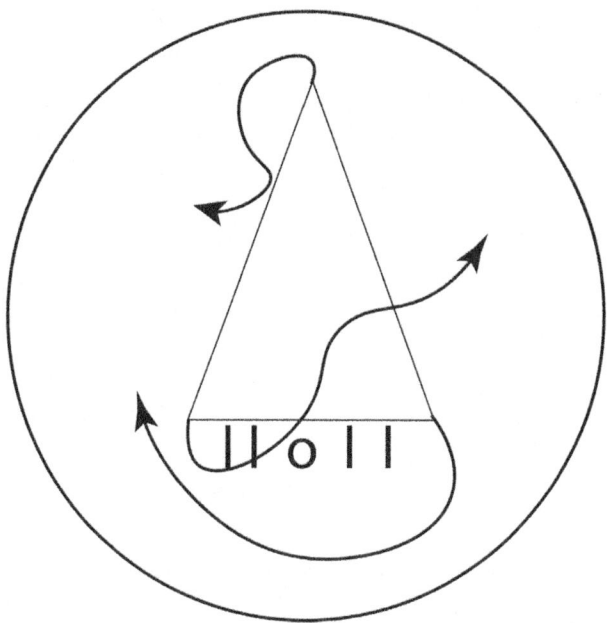

DAVID THOMPSON

286

Satan's Sexuality and Liberation Sigil

Sexuality and Liberation

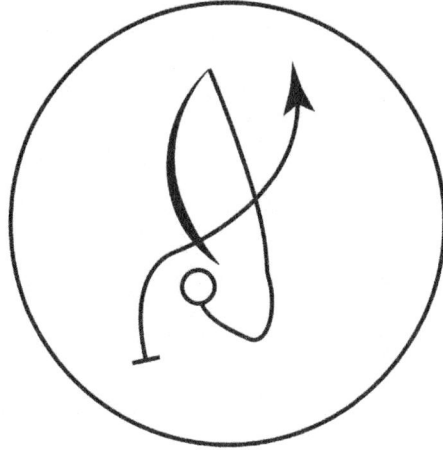

Satan's Egregore Sigil

Satan Egregore

Satan's Balance of Light and Darkness, Transformation Sigil

Balance of Light and Dark

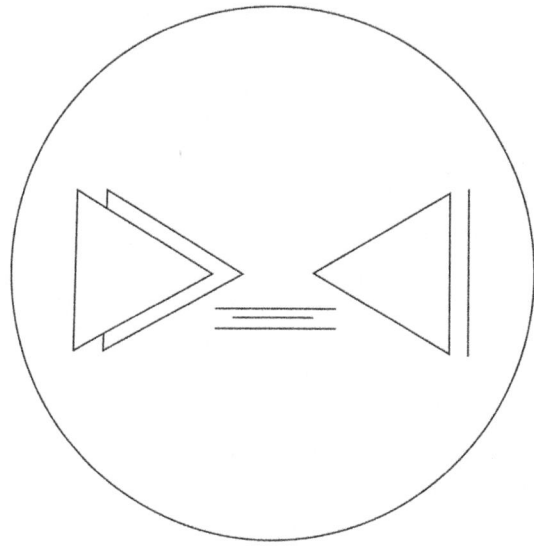

DAVID THOMPSON

Satan's Benevolent Protector & Healing Sigil

Protection

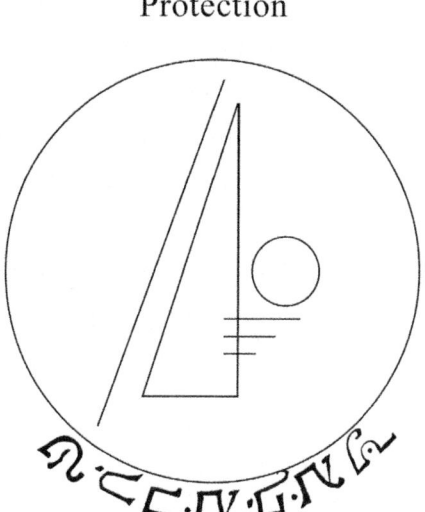

Satan Wealth Sigil

Wealth Mastery

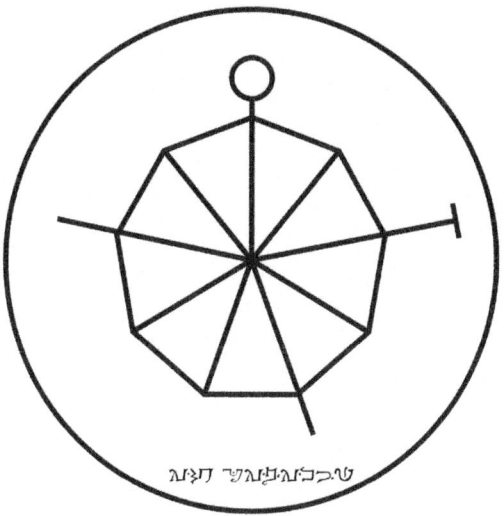

HOW TO USE THE SIGILS

You can download the sigils on my website at:

https://davepsychic.com/satan-book-sigils/

To use, print out and cut apart the sigil you wish to use. Then simply begin using it. These sigils are already "activated" and ready for use, with the aspect of Satan already tied to the specific sigil

ABOUT THE AUTHOR

Dave is an author of adult fantasy (The Furies series) as well as author of occult books about magick.

He began working ritual magick back in the 1970s. He took a brief break, then used the power of this magick to create a photography career which took him to Los Angeles and work as a photographer for multiple magazines.

David has studied magick in all forms, and in 2018, released a three-part magick instruction course in High Magick. Thousands of students have benefited from David's unique teaching style, making ceremonial magick accessible to everyone.

Dave also has a series on Grecian Magick, exploring the aspects of ceremonial magick with the gods and goddesses of ancient Greece.

Magick Books by David Thompson
    Available as EPUB, Paperback and Hardcover (*)

High Magick Series
    High Magick 101
    Daemons of High Magick
    Daemons and the Law of Attraction*
    Magick of Astaroth*

Lilith: Goddess of Darkness and Light*

Daemons of Fortune*

Asmodeus King of Daemons*

Goddesses of High Magick

Protection Magik

The Diviner's Handbook

The Magik of Lucifer*

The Magik of Freya and Frigg

Grecian Magick Series

Magick of Apollo

Magick of Hermes

Magick of Aphrodite

Magick of Fortuna*

Greco-Roman Wealth Magick*

Magick of the Sirens/Magick of the Muses

Hermes and the Akashic Records

Fiction Novels by David Thompson

The Furies Series

Angels of Vengeance

Descent into Tartarus

Furies: Beginnings

Brianna: Making of a Fury

Printed in Dunstable, United Kingdom

66164072R00178